THE WEST

THE WAY IT REALLY WAS!

~ NEVADA ~

By Norm Nielson
Author of *TALES OF NEVADA!*

Introduction by
James W. Hulse

Edited by
Phyllis B. Turner

Other books by Norm Nielson

Reno: The Past Revisited
Tales of Nevada!
Tales of Nevada, Vol. II
Guns along the Comstock

Additional stories are available on an
audio cassette entitled **Tales of Nevada!**

TO MY PARENTS,
DON AND HELEN.
FOR EVERYTHING...

Table of Contents

Introduction

Norm Nielson is a natural story-teller whose gentle, dignified, authoritative voice has become familiar to thousands of radio listeners, television viewers, and banquet audiences across Nevada. He is the best known popularizer of regional history in this corner of the West in our time.

Nielson has found several techniques for transmitting the legends and lore of Nevada's past to audiences beyond the reach of more conventional historians. From scores of diverse sources, he has gathered the anecdotes that have circulated among the annalists of Nevada legends for generations, and now, once again, he has offered them to us in a convenient printed form.

Here is a generous installment of the kind of yarns that were told around the campfire or before the family hearth in days of yore. Today, television has replaced those smokey remnants of a more rustic past, and Nielson has become a media personality of some consequence by virtue of his mastery of such lore. Through his syndicated radio program, he is heard daily by more than one million listeners. Thousands of television viewers have seen him on the tube, charming us with tales sometimes tall and usually soothing, with moralizations ever so gentle. Uncounted legions of others have seen his words in print in *Tales of Nevada!* and can now hear new stories told by the author on cassette tapes entitled *The Best of "Tales of Nevada!"*

In an earlier era, Nell Murbarger and Don Ashbaugh were the foremost popularizers of Nevada history and legend. Both were deservedly respected for awakening in their audiences wider interests in Nevada's heritage. Norm Nielson has replaced their anthologies with his contemporary books, of which this one is the most ambitious. Here one meets again the likes of Joseph Walker the explorer, Sarah Winnemucca the Paiute Princess, "Old pancake" of Comstock Lode fame, the missionaries of the Las Vegas Mormon Fort, and other friendly companions from Nevada's past. Here are stories about ancient Fish Lake and native Americans, stories about the frontiersman's propensity for the consumption of whiskey, stories about the lonely but rewarding world of the sheepherder. For good measure, he has added a few anecdotes and legend-makers from more recent times, including Wildhorse Kitty Wilkins and Lucius Beebe.

All these accounts are short and uncomplicated, as good yarns usually are, and there is no particular pattern to them. There is no need to approach them in any particular order; one can rummage about among them as one does through comfortable old clothes. The emphasis is on soothing diversion, and there is plenty here to satisfy a myriad of tastes. One will find enough variety to engage the attention of every generation and a score of diverse interests.

Occasionally, there are those who like to take their history straight, without the kind of mixers that Nielson adds to his refreshments. As Mark Twain, that master story-teller, once said, there may be a few "stretchers" here, and he perpetrated quite a few himself. But tellers of legends and transmitters of romances have always had the privilege of taking a bit of license and their art is more ancient and more popular than that of the more formal chroniclers and analysts. In Norm Nielson's presence we are encouraged to relax and let the skillful pied piper work his magic.

Jim Hulse
Reno, Nevada
September, 1994

Acknowledgements

I gave a speech to a lovely group of women some time back. They call themselves the Doctor's Wives, and they meet monthly at Washoe Medical Center in Reno. Among other charitable contributions, the group dedicates itself to raising money for worthy causes, scholarships and the like.

But the ladies also have a sense of humor. In my speech I happened to comment on the fact that early Nevada physicians often prescribed whiskey as a universal cure-all. For example, a common cure for dysentery was whiskey mixed with tea. With tongue-in-cheek, I casually blamed today's high rate of alcoholism on frontier doctors.

Well, the following morning there was a package on my desk. Inside, a bottle of whiskey, a package of tea, and a note that read, "In our husbands' continuing tradition...." I was floored. They had put one over on me. They were treating *me* for dysentery. To make matters worse, I had opened the package in front of everyone in my own office. They didn't let me forget it for weeks.

I'm constantly amazed at the caliber of people who have made this land what it is today and the intense pride they seem to have in our state and in our heritage. They are hard-working, high-spirited, and immensely creative. Happily, they are humorous as well. I know. And *The West. The Way It Really Was! Nevada* is the result. I simply take the stories of these amazing people and pass them on to you.

What began as a small radio program more than a decade ago now is heard by more than a million listeners daily. The radio program has spawned weekly and monthly columns, and those columns have turned into a series of books and audio cassettes. Thanks to you, they have been pretty popular.

But this modest success would never have happened without some very special people. Peter Bandurraga, intrepid leader of the

Nevada Historical Society, always reminded me that our vastly interesting history didn't stop with the coming of the motor car; it continues to this day. Don Drake, owner of Yellow and Delux Taxi of Reno, and a history buff himself, sent me over a hundred old newspaper clippings, some of which appear in this volume. Robert Laxalt, Nevada's premier author, continues, as always, to inspire me to write more about people than events. And my lovely wife, Teri, sat through more than seventy-five speeches last year. Somehow, she still managed to give me not only much-needed moral support but also accurate critiques.

Special thanks go to Jim Hulse of the University of Nevada, Reno, whose kind words you have just read. Professor Hulse is nationally acclaimed as one of the west's finest historians, and here in Nevada his books are legend, considered by most to be the premier chronicles of the state's history. I am flattered that he agreed to add his distinguished name to this collection of stories and extremely honored.

But more than anyone else, I must thank Phyllis Turner, whose outstanding editing has made this book possible. You see, once I have written the material for a book, I really hate to look at it anymore. So much has happened in the Silver State that I'm constantly off on the trail of the new and different. The stories I told yesterday, I generally put aside. There is always something entirely new hiding out there somewhere, and I'm determined to find it.

But Phyllis, a former teacher, insisted that we tell the story anyway. She locked herself up for an entire winter, neglecting her horses, her chickens, her goats, her cats, and even her beloved dogs (to say nothing of her husband, David), to massage, to tweak, to clean up a myriad of mistakes and make some sense out of the mumbo-jumbo. As a result, she has created a work of which I am extremely proud.

But most of all, I must thank you, the reader. You see, you are the real heroes of West. If the truth were known, I hardly have to do research any more. Seldom does a week go by that I don't receive something in the mail -- a diary, an old book, a faded clipping -- they are tiny but precious glimpses of the past not found in any museum, not on record in any library. Priceless treasures, every one.

So thank you. Thank you all. Even though I'm running out of storage space, and Teri is ready to kill me, keep those cards and letters coming.

After all, I certainly wouldn't want to run out of material...

Preface

I have a hunch that Nevada is about to go through some pretty tough times.

As I pen these words, Washington is again making noises about raising fees on ranching and increasing the tax on mining, two of the state's most enduring and precious resources. In addition, gambling, the state's largest industry, is being threatened by competition as close as neighboring California. Already Nevada casinos, most notably those in Reno, are seeing a declining "drop," as the daily revenues are called, and although Las Vegas is still in the throes of the biggest building boom in its history, only the larger more theme-oriented properties will probably survive. Without casino revenues, Nevada is going to have to tighten its belt.

But before you accuse me of being a pessimist, listen up. As you will learn from these pages, the revenue problem that looms ominously on the horizon is nothing new. One has only to look at Nevada's past for confirmation.

Like much of the sprawling West, Nevada has always been a boom or bust state. Before silver was discovered near present-day Virginia City, Nevada was little more than a stopping off place on the way to somewhere else. Nevada prospered then, but only for a time.

With the decline of the mines in the late 1870's, Nevada declined as well. In fact, the population actually shrank, so much so that a resolution was introduced on the floor of Congress calling for the revocation of Nevada's statehood. It was unsuccessful.

Nevada's mineral wealth came once more to the rescue. With the rich discoveries in Tonopah and Goldfield, the state again enjoyed the promise of growth and prosperity, only to have its hopes dashed in a few short years when the mines petered out.

In response, Nevadans created a divorce industry to head off another depression, and for a time the concept actually worked. Movie stars, middle eastern princes, and scions of industry flocked to Nevada to shed their spouses. They were offered "secrecy as to details, swanky gambling casinos, horse racing, dude ranches, winter sports amid mountains, fine hotels and a gay night life." Their money also kept Nevada green. But only for a time...

Gambling helped when it was introduced in 1931. But it was not until the Second World War when troop trains bound for the west coast stopped for a little R 'n' R that the age of modern gaming truly began. After the war, those same troops returned, this time to kick up their heels and enjoy what some were calling "Nevada-style fun!" There were "floating" crap games in swimming pools, war planes landed on the Las Vegas Strip, and showgirls appeared au naturel. There was excitement everywhere. The future seemed assured. Bugsy Siegal and the "mob" moved in, but no one seemed to care. After all, Nevada was on a roll again.

But today, after yet another period of prosperity, I think Nevada is in for it one more time. One fine morning in the not too distant future, the state will wake up to find that a huge casino is being built on some Indian reservation just across the border, and panic will set in. Politicians will grieve, grit their teeth, and wonder out loud where the money will come from.

And when that happens, this "optimist" will tell them.

It will come from that strange, wonderful, determined, ingenious group of people that the nation has come to call Nevadans. As this book illustrates, it was not her mineral wealth, her tourism, or her industry which made Nevada great. Even in the best of times, these things were fleeting. It was, instead, her resourceful people, people who were able to carve an oasis in the middle of a desert, to make things grow where nothing had grown before. It will take a little time and a lot of hard work, but Nevadans will make her great again.

That's what living out here in the "Wild West" is all about. It's about making things happen. So prop your feet up and enjoy a few stories from *The West. The Way It Really Was! Nevada*.

Nevada

Though she may be dry as bone
And she may resemble hell
This old Nevada desert
Well, it might be just as well
Cause if she had more water
They would pave her far and wide
And when they got through buildin
There'd be no place left to hide
Not overrun by people
Who think beauty must be wet
Cause if they had the water
There'd be no peace left to get
If it has to come to that
Well, I sure don't have to guess
If it brings crowds and condos
Then I'll settle for less
That she won't float a surf board
Sure don't take no whiz at math
But I don't really care much
Long as I can take a bath
And have enough for coffee
When I wake up in the morn
Yeah, Nevada may be dry
But I have to toot her horn
She's still got room to breathe in
And a silence pure and sweet
And spaces left a plenty
Not covered with concrete
She's got sunset to awe you
And a distance sharp and clean

She ain't like no other place
Anybody's ever seen
But if you like her wet folks
Then she ain't the state for you
Move on up to Oregon
Where they have a heavy dew
Build your condo by the sea
Where the balmy breezes blow
Where they have a hurricane
Every couple years or so
Or there in jolly England
Where they have a constant damp
I know you'll like it there
Just don't desecrate my camp
But if you choose Nevada
I reckon you'll get by
Cause she's got lots to offer
Just don't cuss her cause she's dry

Cowboy Poet
Richard Smith

The Legend of the Pine Nut Trees

The story has been passed solemnly from generation to generation, told in hushed but timeless voices by the scant light of a dwindling fire. Long before the land that would become Nevada saw the coming of the white man, the legend was an integral part of Washoe Indian lore, a tale of famine and pestilence, of Washoe against Paiute, of a benevolent and forgiving god warring against a being that can only be called a devil. No modern language can do it justice, for the Washoe tongue does not translate completely or accurately into English. Still, it is an intriguing story of how Nevada's official tree, the pinion pine, came into being...

Gou-Wet, Coyote God, was a jealous deity. To Nevada's earliest inhabitants he was the devil incarnate, the malevolent force behind all things evil, and he looked down enviously upon the tribes in the valley below.

More than 100 million years before, a powerful eruption had pushed the towering Sierra Nevada skyward from the earth's crust. A lush, protected valley had been created in the shadow of this rugged mountain range; an Eden sprang from the desert sage. The Carson Valley was at peace, shared in harmony by the Washoes and their neighbors, the Paiutes, the Shoshones, and the Diggers.

For as long as any of the elders could remember, the bounty of the valley had been protected by Wolf God. This benevolent being had created a river which wound itself gracefully along the foot of Job's Peak. The river, said Wolf God, was sacred. By bathing in its cleansing waters, sin and disease would be washed away. The Washoes had only to immerse themselves in the gently flowing waters and they would become immortal, said Wolf God, and the tribe would multiply tenfold.

The small valley provided tall, luxurious grasses for warm huts; the surrounding mountains provided protection from the harsh

1

winter snows and wind. The members of the Washoe tribe were plentiful in number and enjoyed an abundance of wild game and rich plant life. All was good.

But Gou-Wet saw the happiness of the tribe, and he was jealous. He vowed to bring chaos to the valley and descended from above.

Calling the tribe together, he assumed his most hideous form, his arms and legs pocked with sores, his hands knarled into claw-like appendages. "Do not wash in the sacred river," he admonished the elders, "or you will take my form. You will become wrinkled, old, and die!" If his words went unheeded, he warned, all the tribes would forget how to use their bows and arrows. Without food they would surely starve. Pulling his horrendous form to its full height, he vowed he would eat those who failed to follow him.

The people of the valley yielded to the words of Coyote God, with disastrous results. No longer did they bathe; they became lazy and shiftless. Children fought with each other. Wild game suddenly became scarce. Famine swept the region, and sickness followed. Women wailed and tore their hair in frustration and fear. In the wake of a mysterious plague, even strong warriors died by the hundreds. Arguments broke out among the tribes. War came. The Paiutes viciously attacked their neighbors, the Washoes, stealing their horses and leaving them on foot. A great fire swept the valley. It burned the precious pine nut trees, long the staple of the Indian diet, to the ground.

But the benevolent Wolf God was watching over the Indians of the valley. In spite of the evil ways to which his people had succumbed, he was a forgiving god. He vowed to go to the aid of the remaining members of the tribe, to provide food for his starving people.

He made thousands of hunting arrowheads and dropped them from the skies, scattering them across the valley for his hungry warriors. But cunning Gou-Wet was watching, and he poisoned the arrowheads. They fell to the ground, but anyone touching them perished instantly.

When Wolf God saw this, he vowed to defeat Coyote God. This time he scattered pine nut seeds across the mountain slopes. The seeds immediately took root and sprang magically into full-grown pinions loaded with precious nourishment. But by now the remaining Washoes were too weak to climb the trees to obtain the life-giving nuts. Again Wolf God came to their rescue. He reached down and placed his giant hand upon the trees and pushed them toward the ground. He shrank the pine nut trees by the thousands, and the Washoes were able to gather the nuts, and so were saved.

Since that time, the Washoes have depended on the pine nut trees for food, and the trees themselves, under the watchful eye of Wolf God, have always remained short.

So ends the legend of Gou-Wet and Wolf God, a timeless story of the creation of one of Nevada's most precious resources, the sturdy, nutritious pinion pine, Nevada's state tree.

Discovering Nevada with Joseph Walker

He was a giant of a man, standing well over six feet with arms capable of snapping a man in two. By the time he had turned twenty-three, he had settled in what were then the far reaches of American civilization, Missouri. He laid out and named the townsite of Independence, served as a sheriff in the region, and then set his sights on the mysterious west. Joseph Walker would forever leave his mark on the land that soon would become known as Nevada.

Joseph Reddeford Walker had been born in the wilds of Tennessee in 1798, at a time when few people realized the great expanse of the American continent. But Walker had a wanderlust; he was always searching for new streams to cross, new mountains to climb. When word began to circulate that an expedition to the far west was being planned, Walker jumped at the chance.

The reason for the expedition is still shrouded in mystery. It was organized by Benjamin Louis Bonneville, an army officer on furlough from the United States Military Academy at West Point. Some say that Bonneville was intrigued by the tremendous potential of the beaver trade in the Rocky Mountains and beyond. Others claim that he was on a secret mission authorized by the United States government to scout foreign lands with an eye on western expansion.

But the reason mattered little to Walker. It was excitement he craved, and within the next few years he would find it beyond measure.

It was July, 1833, when the expedition set out. The Bonneville party was divided into three groups, one under Walker's command. His orders were to explore the region around the Great Salt Lake, then travel west toward the Pacific in search of beaver. If none were found, Walker was instructed to return to Salt Lake for a rendezvous.

According to Zenas Leonard, official clerk and record keeper for the party, Walker was eminently qualified to lead the expedition: "He

5

was well hardened to the hardships of the wilderness, understood the character of the Indians very well, was kind and affable to his men, but at the same time at liberty to command without giving offense, and to explore unknown regions was his delight." With each man outfitted with four horses, two rifles, heavy blankets, buffalo robes, and supplies, they set out on what would become an historic journey.

Negotiating the salt flats along the Great Salt Lake was made easier with the help of several Indian guides, and it wasn't long before Walker and his men had reached the edge of the desert leading into the Great Basin. They came across a river that seemed to go nowhere. Walker, noting the desolation of the land along it, named the river The Barren. [Editor's note: When the Fremont party officially mapped the area some ten years later, Fremont would re-name it the Humboldt River.]

It was along this river that the trials that lay ahead soon became evident. Beaver were scarce. When the men set out their traps, they found them prey to local Indians who stole them at every opportunity. Unknown to Walker, several of his men had shot two Indians they caught stealing the traps, and the party rose one morning to find themselves surrounded by a band that numbered almost one hundred braves.

Walker knew that they could not hope to survive against such numbers, so he ordered his men to fire at some ducks that were feeding among the reeds across the river. The Indians, having never seen firearms before, were stunned when the ducks fell instantly. Walker followed through with another demonstration of the white man's power. He ordered a buffalo robe set up as a target, and, one by one, his men hit their mark at ever-increasing distances. The ruse worked; the Indians withdrew.

But within several days the Indians, now fortified by even greater numbers, returned. This time Walker had no choice. He ordered his men to charge; within minutes, more than thirty braves lay dead along the riverbank. In the confusion of battle, the Walker party was able to head south. They reached the foot of the Sierra Nevada without incident, but by now their food supplies were exhausted.

The Sierra mountain range had never been traversed. Walker was forced to thrust into the Sierra, then retreat, then forge ahead again in an attempt to find a route over the mountains. Exhausted, depressed, and hungry, the men were reduced to eating some of their own horses. At one point, one of them stumbled across a young Paiute who had been collecting pine nuts. The Indian panicked and dropped his basket. The nuts sustained the group for almost a week.

As fate would have it, just as the men were about to give up, they struck the pass for which they had been searching. In the weeks that followed, Walker's party, all suffering from malnutrition, finally triumphed over the treacherous slopes and made their way down into California.

There they came upon giant redwoods. No one had ever even imagined the magnitude of such trees. The men camped in the shelter of the towering sentinels for two weeks until their strength returned. A month later, they arrived at the mission community of Monterey. They tallied the tragic cost of their journey: three men, sixty-four horses, and ten cows; they had also eaten fifteen of their dogs along the way.

The party stayed in Monterey until the winter ended. Then, refreshed and resupplied, they began the return trip to their rendezvous at the Great Salt Lake.

They would find the return just as hair-raising, just as perilous. They became lost in the Nevada desert, then suffered two more attacks by hostile Indians, but they made it. The Walker party was the first to discover a route across the towering Sierra Nevada -- and lived to tell about it.

And along the way, they left their mark. To this day, a Nevada lake and river bear the Walker name. Walker Pass, high in the Sierra of California, bears the name as well. Joseph Walker, mountain man, had left his name indelibly etched upon the land.

Old Greenwood

They called him Old Greenwood for obvious reasons. He was a trapper along the Missouri River as early as 1807. By 1810, he had blazed a trail almost to Oregon. By 1844, when he was hired to lead a group of emigrants to California, he was still going strong. By then he was eighty-one years old.

But age hardly hampered the life of the rugged frontiersman. He knew the far west like the back of his hand, had taken a Crow woman as his wife, and spoke numerous Indian dialects. He was just as at home in the deserts of Nevada as he was in the Rocky Mountains.

It was in the spring of 1844 that Caleb Greenwood set out with a party of eleven wagons from Fort Hall in what today is Idaho. From there the group wound its way southwest to Mary's River, subsequently known as the Humboldt. The region had not yet been inundated by the white onslaught; grass along the river was high and game was plentiful.

At the sink of the river, Greenwood met a lone Indian who told him that his name was Truckee, and he agreed to lead the party across the desert to a lush campground at the foot of the Sierra. There, Truckee told the men, they would find another river and a safe respite before the journey over the high mountains.

Truckee was as good as his word. He led the small party safely across the desert and on to the site of present-day Reno. Before leaving the group in Greenwood's capable hands, he described the best route along the river and up into the high Sierra.

But the route was not made for cumbersome wagons. The river, which Greenwood called the Truckee, after his Indian friend, wound itself like a giant snake along the sharp canyon. Huge boulders blocked their path at every turn, and the men had to dislodge each one before they could proceed. Greenwood proved his ingenuity by devising a method whereby the wagons could be partially dismantled and then raised by ropes up the mountainside. Oxen were pushed, pulled, then hoisted up the steep slopes. By March of the following year, Caleb Greenwood, eighty-one years young, had made the first successful crossing of the Sierra via the Truckee River route. He remained in California only a few weeks before returning to Fort Hall.

In the next few years, Greenwood would offer to lead other parties along the path that he had blazed. At Fort Hall, Greenwood and his three sons counseled numerous pioneers on the hazards of the journey and the importance of avoiding the winter snows. One of the groups, the hapless Donner Party, listened, but chose to disregard the aging trapper's advice. They would pay dearly for that decision.

Caleb Greenwood's honesty was legendary. He had long been a friend to the Indians, and they respected the old man. And for good reason: he honored the lives of the Indians on a par equal to white men, including his own family.

In 1845, Greenwood and his son John left Fort Hall, guiding another wagon train. Once the train was safely on its way, Greenwood left the party, leaving John in command while he returned to the Fort and yet another group of emigrants. Author Elbert Edwards recalled what happened next:

> As John was riding in advance of the wagon train, an Indian suddenly arose from the brush at the side of the road. John's horse was frightened and almost threw the rider from the saddle causing a chorus of boisterous laughter from the emigrants behind him. Enraged by the embarrassment, John drew his gun and when the Indian broke into a run, shot him in the back. John Greenwood, realizing what he had done, abandoned the wagon train and galloped off on the trail to California.
>
> That evening Caleb Greenwood caught up with the party. As he rode into the camp, he announced authoritatively that the man who had shot the Indian must die. One of the drivers spoke up to say, 'Your boy John shot him!'
>
> The old man did not flinch. He called all those present for their testimony of what had happened. After getting all the facts, he announced, 'I'll act as judge of this trial. I order that the murderer of the Indian be killed. Shoot him on site, like a wolf!'

Caleb Greenwood never saw his son again. When word reached John Greenwood that his father had placed a death sentence on him, he wisely stayed in California.

Such was Caleb Greenwood's reputation for honesty and fair play. He continued to guide emigrants safely along the river route through the mountains until he was well into his eighties. Each trip provided new knowledge of the desert and of the treacherous Sierra crossing. That knowledge would be used by countless generations who came after him.

Old Greenwood became a legend in his own time. During a period when settlers were appallingly unprepared for the rigors of the trail, Greenwood saved hundreds of lives. Thanks to the oldest living mountain man, countless emigrants would make it to the "promised land" of California.

Someplace in Between

The Silver State has spectacular scenery, a climate almost without humidity, politicians who usually return phone calls, and, for much of its history, enough valuable minerals have been uncovered from the earth to keep most of the residents off the tax doles. But equally important is the liberal attitude that most folks possess. While the rest of the nation was outlawing various forms of gambling as "sinful" and "the scourge which will surely lead to Hell on earth!", Nevadans were legalizing it with very profitable results. Sin itself was turned into a genuine tourist attraction, a concept that would support the fledgling state when mining booms went bust.

In the early 1800's, however, there was not a single American who was aware of this part of the country, the area that would become known as Nevada. The handful of early trappers that bothered to cross the Mississippi River carefully avoided the desert regions, following instead the larger inland rivers to the north. But the situation would change dramatically by mid-century. In 1846, four major events occurred which would change the future of the United States forever. All of them would have direct effects on Nevada and would prove monumental in their scope.

The first, the War with Mexico, would eventually result in the American acquisition of much of the southwestern United States, including a large portion of what would become Nevada. Next, the western migration of the followers of the Mormon Church would begin the colonization of the region. During that same year the Donner Party would perish as the result of their ill-fated decision to take a little-known Nevada short-cut over the wintry Sierra Nevada rather than the traditional trail to Oregon. Their tragedy and the lurid tales of cannibalism that resulted would focus world-wide attention. The fourth occurrence, an agreement between Great Britain and the United States which created the permanent southern boundary of Oregon, would also have considerable impact in the years to come.

But back in the mid-1800's, the full effects had yet to be felt. In fact, the region was referred to as "an arid land between Zion to the east and the Garden of Eden to the west." That description was not far from wrong. Zion, the popular term for the Mormon Church, was indeed to the east. With headquarters near the Great Salt Lake, Mormon pioneers spread out to "civilize" the region. Early Mormons were the state's first miners, farmers, and developers. They built the first settlements, opened the first trading posts, lined out the first routes through the territory, and received the first government contracts to carry the mail. The Garden to the west, of course, was California. To most Americans it resembled the Biblical land of milk and honey -- the weather was warm, the soil rich, and, to top it off, there were "nuggets of gold just sticking right up out of the ground."

In truth, by the half-century mark, the majority of people in Nevada were just passing through, and the flow of humanity reached record proportions. In 1849, more than 22,000 people made the trek across the Great Basin. By the following year, when word of the California gold strike reached the eastern seaboard, that number more than doubled -- to 45,000 immigrants. By 1852, 52,000 men, women, and children, leading three times as many head of cattle, oxen, horses, and mules, followed the route across what would become Nevada. An incredible number of people were "just passing through."

Inevitably, of course, some people decided to stay. First among them was a Mormon businessman, John Reese. Though not a missionary, Reese was still part of the hearty breed of Mormon pioneers bent on earning a profit, a portion of which would be returned to the Church. He dabbled in trade, in land, even in mining. At a spot just a few miles from the Carson River in the shadow of the Sierra, Reese and his party began construction of the first permanent settlement in the territory. Christened Mormon Station (today it is known as Genoa, and a reconstruction of some of the original buildings may be seen), the tiny assortment of rough-hewn buildings immediately became a beehive of activity.

But Mormon influence would be short-lived. In an 1857 conflict that saw a confrontation between Mormon leader Brigham Young and the United States government, Young called all his followers back to Salt Lake to defend the city against an army which never materialized. Almost overnight, the entire Mormon population disappeared from Nevada.

The settlement of the region would soon have a new messiah, an itinerant Irishman by the name of James Finney. Finney and his partners were searching for gold in the foothills just northeast of

14

Mormon Station and came across not gold, but silver. The strike, named the Comstock Lode, would turn out to be the richest ever recorded. Soon the vast hordes of prospectors and settlers who just a few years earlier had headed west turned east again. The rush this time was not to California, but Nevada. The future, at long last, was assured.

Today people still come to the Silver State hoping to strike it rich, but the barren desert has been covered by a sea of green felt, by steel towers that reach high above the desert floor. The ringing of jackpot bells has replaced the clanging of the pick. The tourist has replaced the prospector, the station wagon and the bus, the trusty mule. Nevada has come a long way, especially since the days when the state was known only as that "Godforsaken" place "between Zion and the Garden of Eden."

The Way It Was

They were times of turbulence but also of dreams. Thousands of Americans, in a desperate attempt to find a new "promised land," were streaming across the country -- by wagon, on horseback, often on foot. The tales of the hardships that awaited were cast aside for accounts of gold to be had for the taking. The westward movement had begun.

They uprooted themselves with a jerk, packed their meager belongings into creaking wagons, and headed west from Independence, Missouri. They survived the endlessness of the Great Plains, the savagery of Indian country. They crossed the impassable Rockies. The end, they thought, was certainly in sight. But their first glimpse of the region that would become known as Nevada would be a rude awakening for most.

Most of the emigrants headed almost due west -- through Kansas, Nebraska, and Wyoming. By the time they had reached the midpoint of Idaho, however, it was decision time. Head northwest and up through the relative safety of Oregon? Turn south through unchartered Nevada to California? For many it was a decision that would end in death.

If they existed at all, the lonely markers along the Humboldt Trail were simple at best. For the most part, they were just a piece of wagon board lashed with rawhide to the trunk of a sage. The inscriptions, carved hastily into the rotting wood, usually contained little more than the sad but lingering truth: "Mary Jane McCelland departed this life, Aug. 18th 1849 aged 3 yrs. 4 mos." As the century neared its halfway point, one diary chronicled 930 such graves along the treacherous route through the infamous Forty Mile Desert.

A description written by William Johnston in 1849 warned, "The valley of the shadow of death. Who enters here, leaves hope behind." The words were ominous but true. By the time most pioneers reached the desert, they had already been on the trail more than three months, and their supplies were seriously depleted. Hunger and thirst were rampant, disease everywhere; heat and fatigue took their toll.

Many who perished were nameless. Wrote one traveller, John Steele, back in 1850: "They were buried in shallow graves, the earth heaped above them and a stake bearing the single word 'unknown' placed at the head." Pioneer Charles Furguson, who buried one of his companions during that same year recalled, "The poor fellow was a stranger to us. We had met him upon the start and none of us knew his name or the address of his mother. The labor and anxiety of such a journey are so exhausting to the body and absorbing to the mind that we rarely get the name of an associate, much less knowledge of his history and family."

The young were usually taken first. "About midnight," wrote John Clark, "our neighbor approached our campfire and told us that his only child had just died and he had come to solicit aid to bury it. We promised that in the morning his wants would be attended to." The next morning, they took "an empty cracker box which we made answer for a coffin, dug a grave in the middle of the road and deposited the dead child therein. The sun had just risen and was a spectator to that mother's grief as she turned slowly but sadly away from that little grave to pursue the long journey yet before her. We filled the grave with stones and dirt and when we rolled out we drove over it. Perhaps we had cheated the wolf by doing so. Perhaps not."

Not all such attempts to avoid the scavengers were successful. "Coming down from this stream we have seen the skulls of a number of persons who have been buried in '49, '50, and '51," wrote R.H.P. Snodgrass the next year; "[They] have been dug up by wolves and their bones left to whiten the plains." Mournfully he added, "We see a great many fresh graves of the victims of this year."

Though it seems inconceivable today, many persons too ill to travel were simply abandoned during the crossing. G.W. Thissell came across one such hapless adventurer in 1849: "Found a man dead by the roadside today. Two stakes were driven into the ground and over them was drawn a piece of wagon sheet under which the man lay. By his side was a cup of water and a piece of hard bread." Apparently the victim had not been dead long. Beside the body was a card which read, "please give this man a cup of water and bread if he needs it. He was not able to travel and wanted to be left."

Often entire families were claimed by Nevada's desert. Wrote John N. Lewis in 1852: "Mrs. Barnes died at half past nine. Amandy was taken sick this morning and died in the afternoon. Mahala was taken this morning and is not likely to recover." As an afterthought, he continued sadly, "The three women were sisters."

Despite the hardship, there were many who made it, though more than a few seemed to do so almost in spite of themselves, armed only with blind faith. One case in point was the Bidwell-Bartleson party. John Bidwell was a schoolteacher who knew little about the region that lay ahead. They had no guide and set out in the company of some Jesuit missionaries. The first part of the journey was uneventful, but by the time the wagon train had reached Fort Hall in Idaho, the group split up. The missionaries continued north to Oregon, and the Bidwell party -- consisting of thirty-two men, one woman, and a child -- continued bravely south into the forbidding desert. The woman, Nancy Kelsey, was barely eighteen, yet already a wife and mother. When given the option of continuing on in the relative safety of the Jesuits, she chose instead to stay with her spouse, claiming, "Where he goes I go. I can better endure the hardships of the journey than the anxieties of an absent husband." Her persistence and fortitude paid off. Kelsey and her daughter were the first women to cross the territory in safety.

So it was in early Nevada. The number of people who lost their lives in the desolate wilderness is awesome. By some estimates more than 3,000 people died in the years 1849-1852.

Today, of course, many travellers cross the desert on asphalt highways in air-conditioned cars and motor homes. Perhaps they should pause for a bit and think, to remember those who came before -- particularly those who died in the attempt.

They Started It All

One was Allen, the other Hosea. They were well-educated as prospectors went, the sons of a Universalist clergyman, A.B. Grosch, who edited a religious newspaper in the town of Utica, in upstate New York. Both had studied metallurgy before coming west; unlike most of the seekers, the Grosch brothers knew what they were looking for. They would find it too, although their story, a tale of one of the richest strikes on earth, would end in poverty and death.

It was 1852. In the camp that was called Johnstown (now Dayton) on the slopes of Mount Davidson, the Grosch brothers alternated between working and going hungry, between back-breaking labor and impending starvation. For a while, they would move slowly, painstakingly up the slopes of the towering mountain. In desperation, they would return to California and work at other tasks, trying to put together a grubstake. Then they would go back again to the area known as Gold Canyon.

The canyon was living up to its name, though sparingly. For more than two years, eager miners, tired of eking out a precarious existence in the declining gold fields of California, had been finding good color among the sagebrush strewn arroyos. A Big Bonanza was ahead. They were sure of it. There were no big strikes yet, of course. But they were out there somewhere. They just knew it.

They were a motley crew -- an odd lot, those men of Gold Canyon. In addition to the young brothers, there was a lazy teamster, James Fennimore. Sometimes called James Finney, other times referred to as "Old Virginny," he would later lend his name to Virginia City. There were the Irishmen, Peter O'Reilly and Pat McLaughlin. The strangest of the lot was a gregarious fellow by the name of Comstock. "Old Pancake," they called him, for his affinity for flapjacks.

But while the rest of the men were bent on finding that elusive outcropping of gold, the Grosch brothers were convinced that the ore in the area was deeper, underground. And they were not convinced that all that glittered was gold at all. For months, most of the miners had been confounded by a bluish substance that they referred to as "that infernal blue stuff." Others had been throwing the "stuff" away, exasperated because it stuck to their pans while they were washing for gold, cursing it because it got in their way. But the brothers, with their metallurgical background, knew better. They had a hunch that the "stuff" was actually sulfuret of silver. They were convinced they were on to something. In September of 1856, after coming across two giant veins, they were sure. They wrote home excitedly, "We have discovered the perfect monsters!"

But the trouble was, no one was paying attention, not at the diggings, not even over in California. Armed with samples of the vein, the men journeyed over the Sierra to an assayer. The sample proved almost worthless. Still the brothers would not give up.

They made the rounds trying to scrounge up enough backing to mount a full-scale working of their find. They were turned back time and time again. "Too expensive," came the reply. "Quartz mining is just too risky, it requires too much machinery." Discouraged but unwilling to give up, the Grosch brothers returned once more to Gold Canyon.

But while they were back in Nevada trying their best to find other elusive veins, something extraordinary was happening in California. At the office where they had deposited their samples, another assayer, quite by accident, happened across the strange rocks. Curious, he made an assay of his own. What he learned would make history. He discovered that the first assay had been false, that the quartz samples were actually almost pure silver. They weighed out at an incredible $3,000 a ton! While the unwitting brothers, now close to starvation, continued to scour the desolate canyons, throughout northern California the word was spreading. "On to Washoe!" was the cry.

But the brothers were not to gain by the new discovery. Ignorant of the report of the second assay, they were still working their claim when Hosea Grosch struck his foot with a pick. Blood poisoning set in. Within days he died in their bleak stone cabin at the entrance to American Flat Ravine.

After burying his brother, Allen Grosch set out once again for California. He was armed with new samples, each he believed much richer that the last. He was convinced that this time he had truly struck it rich. But it was not to be. This time it would be Mother Nature, not fate, that would step in.

It was November when Grosch and a companion, Richard Bucke, headed west. A blizzard caught up with them right at the summit. After weeks of wallowing in the chest-deep whiteness, blinded by the driving snow, their food supply ran out. At night they burrowed deep into the drifts for warmth. In desperation they killed their donkey and ate it. Suddenly, the storm ended. At long last the men stumbled into a snow-covered mining camp on the western slope. They were safe.

While he rested from his ordeal, Allen Grosch heard the rumors. He learned of the fabulous strike up in Nevada, of silver so pure that it was unbelievable. Allen Grosch suddenly realized that the strike was his, that he was rich, that the years of struggle had finally paid off. But his elation would be short-lived. His feet had been frozen in the raging blizzard. Agonizing and deadly, frostbite had set in. Within twelve days the surviving Grosch brother, heir to one of the greatest finds in the history of America, was dead.

But it mattered little in Nevada. In Gold Canyon the rush was on. Mines were established. The area staked out by the brothers soon became Ophir ground. On another claim, the Gould and Curry mine would spring up. The Grosch brothers were forgotten.

Today, the fabulous strikes that secured the future of Nevada and gave the state the nickname the "Silver State" are still remembered. Almost overnight, the mountains and deserts of Nevada were on the lips of everyone in the nation.

But it never would have happened without the tenacity of two determined young men who refused to call it quits. Allen and Hosea Grosch, though they never lived to see it, had truly started it all.

The Las Vegas Mission

Nevada owes much to the Mormons. Early Mormon settlers carved a route through southern Nevada, a route that wound precariously from Salt Lake, through Death Valley, and on to the Pacific Coast. Meanwhile, others were on the move in the north. There they established the state's first permanent settlement, a trading post called Mormon Station, now the site of Genoa. While a great many pioneers were simply passing through Nevada on the way to someplace else, followers of the Mormon Church were putting down roots, an unheard of situation for the times.

It began with William Bringhurst, who, with his party of thirty men, built a small fort at the site of present-day Las Vegas. Bringhurst was the vanguard of Mormon leader Brigham Young's elaborate plan to establish a string of missions linking the Mormon capital of Salt Lake City with the Pacific Coast. Young hoped to create a prosperous trade route that would safely supply Salt Lake with both supplies and converts.

One of the first Mormon settlers, Lorenzo Brown, was ambivalent in his first reaction to the new desert mission: "This at first seems a pretty location and after crossing a fifty mile desert seems almost a paradise," he wrote, "but after looking around and seeing so little prospect of making a living [it] seems disheartening and if some of the boys get homesick, I could not blame them much."

But settler John Steele recalled in his diary that, at least at first, the plans for the new settlement went well: "The corn finally grows and President Bringhurst has got his mess house up 14 feet high." Several weeks later, on September 30, 1855, he wrote, "The corn is ripening very fast. Melons, pumpkins and squash are ripening very fast. The horses are beginning to fatten up. The fort wall is one third of the way around the fort and progressing. The Indians continue very friendly...."

The work continued. Another settler noted, "The brethren have made great progress having been here just one year today. They have fenced 150 acres of land and cultivated it. Built a fort of adobe 160 feet square, two feet thick and 12 feet high...."

In the spring of 1856, Mormon leader Brigham Young sent Nathaniel Jones to prospect for industrial metals in the region. Jones began his survey along the Colorado River but found nothing of great interest. However, a short time later an Indian led Jones to an outcropping on a prominent mountain, now known as Mount Potosi, and there a supply of lead was unearthed.

That's when the trouble began.

Jones had carried a message from Brigham Young authorizing him to commandeer members of the original settlement if a valuable ore discovery was made. Bringhurst balked, claiming that he needed the men to work the farms and orchards that were now prospering. Jones, with the backing of the church leaders, forced farmers to become miners. Wrote Lorenzo Brown, "for any man to start a company to dig lead when there was not a man in it that ever saw a lead mine or smelting furnace and hardly knew ore when they saw it was perfect nonsense and I expressed my mind before starting."

But start they did. It was the first underground mining ever attempted in Nevada, and it was hazardous at best. The discovery had been made high on the mountain, necessitating the building of a winding road which often succumbed to landslides. Local Indians were hired to bring the ore to the valley floor, but after a single trip, the Indians, finding the labor not to their liking, silently faded away into the desert.

The feud between Bringhurst and Jones continued. Bringhurst refused to let the mission's blacksmith go to the mine, where his expertise in forging tools was sorely needed. He also held up much-needed supplies of flour, which infuriated miner Jones.

Morale near the mine was devastated, but some managed to keep their sense of humor. Wrote one of the workers, "Last night for supper had pancakes and tea, for dinner we had tea and pancakes, so we had a variety." However, when it was learned that Jones was dining each evening on pork and butter, tensions rose.

Bringhurst continued to plant and harvest his crops, offering little assistance to Jones' operation on the slopes of Mount Potosi. Supplies ran so low that Lorenzo Brown requested permission to sell some of his tools to buy wheat for his family. When Jones rejected his request, dissension among the workers grew, and the grievances began to mount. When it was learned that Jones had contracted to produce lead and then conscripted the labors of his men without compensation,

it was the beginning of the end for the mining operation.

Open conflict between the original Bringhurst party and the miners under Jones ensued, each accusing the other of acting in his own interests rather than in the interests of the Church. Wrote historian Elbert Edwards, "It became apparent that there were two ideologies represented -- that of a traditional strict rule by President Bringhurst and the other colonists, and the more liberal views held by the newcomers that supported Jones."

By January of 1857, Mormon leader Brigham Young had enough. Realizing that the spirit of the mission had been broken, he ordered all of his Mormon followers, miners and farmers alike, to return to Salt Lake City.

The grand experiment had come to an end. But little did the early settlers realize what future they had carved for the region. The lead mine at Mount Potosi would become extremely productive during World War I. After the building of Boulder Dam (later renamed Hoover Dam) in the 1930's, the city of Las Vegas, born on the site of an abandoned Mormon mission, became the entertainment capital of the world.

What's in a Name?

Think back to the days of the Comstock Lode; some legendary names immediately come to mind, names like Peter O'Reilly and Pat McLauglin, the original owners of the Ophir claim. James Fennimore is remembered as Old Virginny; Virginia City was named after him. And Henry Comstock, he was the man who lent his name to the biggest strike in United States history. But few remember the name of Herman Camp, a fellow who could have made a bigger fortune than any of them. Herman once owned a piece of the original Comstock; had things turned out differently, it might be Camp who is remembered today instead of the wily Henry Comstock.

It was July of 1859, when Camp first drifted into Virginia City. Like many of the men there, he was not particularly knowledgeable about the fabulous wealth yet to be uncovered, but Camp figured that he had as good a chance as any man to strike it rich -- if he could just find the right claim.

He began by going into the construction business. Soon he had several contracts for some single-story stone buildings. Although a town had yet to be laid out, Camp prospered, for lodging was at a premium. But he still wanted to buy into a lucrative claim, so it's no wonder that, when he heard that none other than was looking for a buyer for his share of the original Ophir claim, Camp immediately sought out the eccentric miner.

Henry Comstock, illiterate and not much given to work, had been one of the first to reach the slopes of Mount Davidson, but it was probably by pure chicanery that he owned any property at all. Rumor had it that he had cheated O'Reilly and Mclaughlin out of portions of their claim in return for some vague water rights. Regardless, when word of the fabulous strike was announced to the world, Comstock gave up working his claim and spent most of his time wandering up and down the mountain bragging to all who would listen that he had

29

"started it all." Although Comstock actually owned very little, he managed to convince many of the newcomers that he owned the entire lode, that he was the "King of the Comstock." Tenderfoot and seasoned prospector sought him out for advice, and he routinely struck deals with newly-arrived investors, offering land that was not even his own.

Still, by fair means or foul, he did own part of what would eventually become the richest claim in the region, the Ophir, and Camp was able to strike a deal with Comstock. The specifics of his sale of the Ophir to Camp are not recorded. It is known that only a single dollar changed hands on August 6, 1859, and the two men concluded their deal with the customary handshake. Herman Camp was now an owner of a controlling interest in the Ophir! He was jubilant as he left the meeting, convinced that he was about to become fabulously wealthy.

Comstock began to have second thoughts. That evening, sitting around a campfire where whiskey flowed freely, he began to think that perhaps he shouldn't have sold his claim. So, armed with liquid courage, he persuaded several of his companions to return to the Ophir to take control of the property again, by force if necessary.

The following morning, Herman Camp arrived at his newly-purchased claim and was astonished to find it in the hands of a group of grizzled and armed prospectors. They threatened to shoot him if he didn't withdraw. Faced with rifles and shotguns, Camp hesitated only a moment before returning to the safety of his cabin. He had a legal contract for his purchase; he had even put a dollar down to seal the deal. He was perfectly within his rights, he reasoned. But how could he confront armed claim jumpers?

In the mining camps, it was customary for men who had disagreements concerning their rights to submit the matter to a group of their peers, other miners who would act as judge and jury, both parties agreeing to abide by the outcome. Camp, feeling that his case was ironclad, never hesitated. He decided to put his fate into the hands of his fellow prospectors.

Friends advised against the miners' court. After all, they suggested, wasn't Comstock one of the most influential men on the Divide? Didn't he boast a following that included more than half the men on the Comstock? Even Dr. Henry DeGroot, one of the first arrivals in the region and a student of both law and medicine, advised against it. "Take your claim to Genoa and file it," he advised. He further recommended that Camp then flee the territory, leaving the matter for the courts to decide.

But Camp was a man who believed in justice. What miner could look the other way when presented with a legal document? He overestimated the character of and his friends.

On the day the miners' court was scheduled to convene, Comstock offered free whiskey to all those who would testify in his behalf. By the time the court began, even those who would not be called to testify had turned into an unruly mob, brandishing weapons, cursing Camp as an outsider who had tried to cheat Comstock out of his claim. Tensions were high when Camp stepped forward to explain his side of the story, and he was drowned out by raucous jeers. When he attempted to present his written agreement, menacing guns appeared. Within minutes, the angry crowd found in favor of .

According to DeGroot, "As had been foreseen, this meeting, when it came to assemble, was made up of Comstock's cronies, a whiskey-sodden set, whose having already prejudiced the case, decided as a matter of course against Camp, who, in accordance with his pledged word, surrendered his deed and gave up the contest. In relinquishing the claim to this property, the acquisition of a splendid fortune was defeated when already within his grasp."

Camp would have the last laugh, if only temporarily. While McLaughlin, O'Reilly, Old Virginny, and even eventually died broke, Herman Camp later acquired an interest in another rich claim, the Gould and Curry. As fate would have it, however, even this rich claim did not pan out for Camp. A series of poor investments eventually left him broke as well.

Still, it is interesting to note that, for a time, Herman Camp had in his possession a deed from , a deed that could have made him the richest miner in Nevada. And who knows, if he had succeeded in keeping his original agreement with , perhaps today Nevadans would be calling the site where it all began "The Fabulous Camp Lode."

Naw; somehow it just doesn't have that ring to it...

Orphans Preferred

WANTED -- Young, skinny, wiry fellows not over 18.
Must be expert riders willing to risk death daily.
Orphans preferred.

The preceding is an ad placed by W.H. Russell in newspapers along the frontier as a prelude to a marvelous undertaking that stirred the imagination of an entire nation. More than eighty select men, most of them small and athletic, barely out of their teens, dashing headlong across the endless expanse of desert, braving the searing heat and bitter cold, outrunning hostile Indians, fording raging streams -- all to deliver the United States mail -- this conjures an image quite unlike any other in our history; it is the stuff of which legends are made.

The legend began in 1859, when Senator William M. Gwin of California met William Russell, the senior partner in Russell, Majors & Waddell, a firm which operated a stageline from St. Joseph, Missouri to Salt Lake City, Utah. Gwin begged Russell to consider running a string of mail riders over the route from St. Joseph to Sacramento. Such a line, Gwin explained, manned by skilled young riders, would link California with the rest of the nation. Persuasively, Gwin pointed out that Russell's firm already was operating a profitable stagecoach route through much of the region; his company knew the terrain; they would be ideal for the job. In addition, the Senator noted, the matter of patriotism could not be overlooked: the United States could scarcely afford to leave California isolated if the colonization of the rest of the continent was ever to be completed.

By the end of the evening, Russell was convinced. Without consulting his partners, he pledged to Gwin that he would survey the route and agreed with the Senator that individual riders could cut the mail time by as much as seventy-five percent. Gwin, satisfied that his native state had secured a vital communications link with the East, returned to California.

But when Russell arrived at his company headquarters, he was dismayed to learn that, despite his grandiose plans, his partners were less than enthusiastic. The route could never be profitable, he was told; individual riders could never carry enough mail. Besides, wasn't the government working feverishly to complete the transcontinental telegraph line, an accomplishment that would doom the future of the dashing Express? Nonetheless, the route was surveyed. But by the time the project was laid out, even Russell was convinced that the concept of a Pony Express would be a financial disaster.

Still, Russell, Majors & Waddell agreed to honor Russell's handshake agreement with Senator Gwin. Knowing full well that the Pony Express might be good for the country but deadly for business, they agreed to launch the venture just the same. On April 3, 1860, the first Pony Rider rode into history.

It was a monumental undertaking. The Express required more than 500 horses and 190 way stations along the overland route. Although the pay, as much as $120.00 a month, was extraordinary for the times, the life of a rider was hardly glamorous. The stretch across Nevada was the roughest challenge of all. Food and other provisions had to be shipped across the endless miles. The barren terrain fluctuated between searing heat and bitter cold and was inhabited by roving bands of Indians already angered by white immigration. Flash floods plagued the territory; wind storms blinded both men and horses. Still, when advertisements soliciting men appeared in Carson City newspapers, more than fifty answered the call.

Each man selected took an oath. Placing his hand on a Bible, each rider recited, "Before the great and living God, during my engagement and while I am an employee of Russell, Majors & Waddell, I will, under no circumstances, use profane language; that I will drink no intoxicating liquors; that I will not quarrel or fight with any other employee of the firm; and that in every respect I will conduct myself honestly, be faithful to my duties and so direct all my acts as to win the confidence of my employers. So help me God." The ceremony competed, each man was given the Bible on which he had pledged his oath. He would carry the book with him on every ride.

The work was exhausting and the conditions left much to be desired. In 1860, the terrain near the station at Sand Springs in Churchill County was described: "Sand Springs deserves its name. The land is combered here and there with drifted ridges of the finest sand, sometimes 200 feet high and shifting before every gale. The water near this vile hole is thick and stale with sulphery salts; it blistered even the hands."

34

If the wilderness was bad, the accommodations provided for the men were even worse: "The station house is no unfit object on such a scene, roofless and chairless, filthy and squalid, with a smoky fire in one corner, impure floor; the walls open to every wind and the interior full of dust. The employees all loitered and sauntered about like cretins. All but one, who lay on the ground crippled and apparently dying by the fall of a horse upon his breastbone."

As if the terrain and living conditions weren't bad enough, there were Indians. When the war against the Paiutes was at its height, J.G. Kelly, assistant station keeper at Cold Springs, reported, "one of our riders, a Mexican, rode into camp with a bullet hole through him from the left to right side...shot by Indians coming down Edwards Creek. He was tenderly cared for, but died before surgical aid could reach him."

Some were luckier, some not. It was 1861 when Indians attacked the station at Dry Creek. Ralph Rosier, the station keeper, was immediately scalped, his body mutilated. John Applegate, a rider, was seriously wounded. Si McCandless, alone in his nearby trading post, heard the commotion and ran for the express station, joining McCandless and rider Bolly Bolwinkle. The three barricaded themselves with sacks of grain while the Indians continued to loot the outbuildings. Applegate, fearing that the end was near, shot himself rather than wait for the torture he was convinced would come. That left McCandless and Bolwinkle, two men against more than thirty armed warriors.

Determined not to join Applegate, the men decided to make a run for the nearest Pony Express station twelve miles away. Under the cover of darkness, they set out. When the Indians discovered the men had escaped, they followed them for several miles, firing into the night whenever a silhouette appeared. After a few hours, the pursuers, tired of the game, returned to burn the Dry Creek station. McCandless and Bolwinkle ran on into the night. The following day they arrived at the next station, their ordeal over. The two men had run twelve miles across the desert. The feet of Bolly Bolwinkle were so torn by the terrain that he was unable to walk for more than a year afterward. Still, they were alive.

The Pony Express rode into being on April 3, 1860; in October of the following year, it rode into history. Although colorful, larger-than-life characterizations appeared in dime novels, periodicals, and newspapers across the country, the life of the Pony Express rider was perilous at best, but that's how legends are made...

The Legend of Emmet McCain

The Pony Express Rider: young and daring, willing to ride through unchartered terrain at breakneck speed, constantly braving danger from raging storms, searing heat, and marauding Indians. Most were barely out of short pants when they volunteered to undertake what was regarded by most as an impossible mission: to carry the United States mail over 2,000 miles of some of the roughest territory in the west -- all for about $100 a month. And a Bible.

Emmet McCain was just such a man. In reality, he was little more than a boy, standing less than 5'4" in his stocking feet, tipping the scales at just over 100 pounds. It was the ideal weight for the job. Within a few short months, Emmet McCain, barely into his teens, would give his life for the Pony Express.

It was the spring of 1861 when young Emmet cinched up his mount in the courtyard of Fort Churchill. The newly erected outpost, built as a protection against hostile Indians, boasted equally green recruits who joked with the youngster as he anxiously awaited the arrival of the rider from the west.

The famous battle of Pyramid Lake had occurred less than a year before; as recently as the previous month there had been a minor skirmish with roving bands of Paiutes along the Humboldt. Nevertheless, McCain, if he considered the reports at all, seemed casually unaware of any impending danger. Though rumors had been circulating about a new Indian uprising, the boy was amazingly calm. "He had nerves made of tempered iron," some of the bluecoats would later recall.

Suddenly, there it was, a cloud of dust on the horizon. McCain mounted his horse and urged it to the mouth of the courtyard. Over a rise burst the relay rider. McCain moved outside the walls and waited, his horse now dancing nervously in anticipation. Quickly the rider came abreast and tossed the mochila to McCain. With a whoop and a holler, Emmet McCain spurred his horse toward the knolls to the east. Within minutes, he had disappeared. He would never be seen alive again.

Historians have been able to piece together most of what happened next. McCain had ridden less than five miles from the fort when smoke signals could be seen on the ridges in front of him. Without breaking his horse's stride, McCain turned south, intent on riding around the ominous signs in the distance.

It was then that other signals began to appear. Reining in his horse, Emmet McCain realized that, if the billowing smoke was any indication, he was almost totally surrounded by hostile Indians. Still, there was little he could do but continue on his ride across the vast desert. The miles began to melt under the hooves of his lathered horse as man and rider dashed through the dense sagebrush, across wide plateaus, in and out of hidden gullies. Finally, McCain had less than ten miles to go until he reached the safety of the next way station.

But as he rounded a bend at the base of a deep arroyo, they appeared, more than thirty armed and well-mounted warriors. Frantically, McCain wheeled his horse and retraced his path; at the end of the arroyo, another band appeared. This time McCain reined in; he was hopelessly trapped. Quickly he grabbed a green switch from a nearby tree, and, turning his horse into the setting sun, he applied the whip wildly, forcing the animal up the embankment. He rode off again, this time directly across the desert.

After another mile, he came to a small wash where the ground appeared to be soft and muddy, the remains of some silent, underground spring. Quickly, McCain dismounted and began digging feverishly with his hands. When he had made a shallow hole, he threw the mochila into it and covered his precious mail. Walking his horse back and forth over the ground to obliterate the tell-tale signs of his digging, McCain leaped on his horse. From the approaching dust cloud, he knew the Indians were only a few hundred yards behind him now. Hastily, he jammed his green switch into the ground to mark the spot and rode off once more into the desert in a last-ditch effort to escape.

Other bands of Paiutes began to close in, shooting. McCain returned their fire, but with every Indian he felled, two more appeared to take his place. Then his horse collapsed with a violent scream. McCain wrenched his leg from under the dying animal and scurried behind its belly. The Indians rode down upon the helpless Pony Rider; within minutes he was dead.

When a troop of calvary arrived the following day, they found the body of young Emmet McCain, bullet-riddled and stripped naked.

Perhaps out of respect for his courage, the boy had not been mutilated. Silently the troopers buried him and backtracked to recover the mail pouch.

The mochila wasn't difficult to locate. It was buried less than a foot deep, Emmet McCain's green switch still sticking out of the mud. The soldiers recovered the pouch and returned to Fort Churchill.

But the story doesn't end there. Legend says that the green switch, the one that McCain had used to whip his horse to flight, the same green switch that he used to mark the location of his valuable mail pouch, took root in the mud and grew into a giant cottonwood tree, a living testimony to the courage of a young Pony Express Rider who rode off to death and glory, a silent marker to his courage.

Today, in the middle of the Nevada desert, such a tree actually exists. A lone cottonwood spreads its cool shade across the searing alkali, providing a welcome respite for the weary traveler. More than 130 years after young Emmet McCain met his fate, the region where it stands is known as the Lone Tree District of Churchill County.

Is that lone tree the same one that Emmet McCain hastily jammed into the mud that fateful day? Does that giant tree mark the spot where the courageous rider hid his valuable mail pouch, the pouch for which he died? Legend says so.

Of course, the story *is* only a legend...

The Creation of a Territory

It had been a long and arduous process. For more than four years, Congress had been inundated with letters, newspaper articles, and the pleadings of politicians: create a separate territory for the citizens of Washoe. But Congress had resisted. The Civil War was raging; the attention of Washington was decidedly elsewhere. Besides, the population of Washoe was mostly made up of itinerant miners, prospectors, and fortune hunters, newcomers who had suddenly rushed in at the announcement of a silver strike on the slopes of Mount Davidson. It was presumptuous, some thought, for treasure hunters to even consider themselves worthy of a separate territory.

The pressure on President Buchanan was enormous. Rumors were circulating that if Nevada were refused the right to establish a new territory, the people of Washoe might enlist the aid of the rebellious South to break away from Utah. It was a ruse, of course, but it worked. On March 2, 1861, two days before he relinquished his presidency to a young lawyer from Illinois, Buchanan signed "An Act to Organize the Territory of Nevada."

But the problems were just beginning. First, boundaries had to be agreed upon. It was suggested that the new territory be bordered by Oregon on the north, by the 37th parallel (the New Mexico Territory) on the south, and that the eastern boundary be the 39th degree of longitude. The western border, however, was in dispute. In the interest of brevity, Congress had suggested that Nevada's western border should be "the dividing ridge separating the waters of the Carson Valley from those that flow into the Pacific...." In other words, the very crest of the Sierra Nevada.

There was a hitch, however. The western border would be confirmed if, and only if, "California should consent to the same." California, realizing that Nevada would be usurping a considerable amount of land, including the spectacular Lake Bigler, today's Lake

41

Tahoe, declined. Despite the cajoling of the people of Washoe, the western border of the new territory remained the same as it had been during the original Utah boundary disputes a decade earlier.

By now Abraham Lincoln had arrived in the White House. Realizing the political expediency of rewarding those who had helped him win the election, Lincoln moved swiftly to pay his debts. To serve as the new governor of the Nevada Territory, he selected James Nye of New York. Although Nye had originally supported William Seward for the Presidency, when Lincoln won the nomination, Nye wisely threw his support behind him and worked tirelessly for Lincoln's election.

It would be a while before the new governor could take up residency in Carson City. It took almost four months for Nye to travel to Panama, then overland, then on to San Francisco by steamship. There, perhaps as a sign of the difficulties that lay ahead, Nye had to wait almost two weeks for his baggage and presidential papers to catch up with him.

On July 8th, Nye finally arrived in Carson City to a welcoming barrage of cannon fire. He began a tour of inspection beginning in Virginia City, by now the largest town in his new domain. There flags were unfurled and a two mile long parade greeted him.

Nye would witness the lawlessness of Nevada on his very first day. A raucous young tough, perhaps suffering from too much John Barleycorn, persisted in firing his sidearm into the air, dangerously close to the reviewing stand occupied by the Governor. When ordered by a deputy to throw down his weapon, the would-be gunslinger challenged the lawman to a shootout. The deputy succeeded in disarming him with well-placed bullets to the man's shoulder and kneecap.

But soon the pomp and circumstance had faded, and Nye settled in for the duration. The immediate problem was the unrest that had been fomenting among Nevada's Indian tribes. For years, Nevada's Indians had been friendly, but as the oncoming hordes of white settlers began denuding the territory of the precious pine nut trees and running off the wild game, a confrontation loomed.

Nye immediately called for a meeting with tribal leaders. Chief Winnemucca of the Paiutes and 400 of his warriors gathered for two days of talks with the new white leader. Indian braves danced across red hot coals to show their strength and determination. Nye responded by turning on his considerable charm. Mark Twain recalled that Nye would "beam on them by the hour out of his splendid eyes and fascinate them with his handsome face and comfort them with his persuasive tongue...till he took all the war spirit out of them and sent

42

them away with his inspired mendacity."

Although he was considered an "outsider," a strange description considering that most residents of the new Territory had been around less than two years themselves, Nye continued to win over his detractors. But he would face problems more difficult than anyone had imagined.

For one thing, the population of the Nevada Territory had grown by more than 10,000 people since it had been organized. Most of the arrivals, with the exclusion of the Indians, were transient, moving from town to town as a new strike was announced, as a new discovery was made. It would be difficult to control such a population, almost impossible to collect any taxes.

Operating capital was another problem. Not realizing the vast distances between major towns and the lack of roads and other forms of travel and communication, the United States Congress had hardly appropriated anything with which to operate the government. In fact, the entire budget for the first year was a scant $20,000, an amount, reported Mark Twain, that was hardly enough "to run a quartz mill for a month," let alone an entire territory.

To the rescue of Nye and his government came Abe Curry, a prominent Carson City businessman who had first laid out the town several years before. The prosperous Curry loaned the financially strapped legislature a stone building on the edge of town, rent-free. He even constructed a horse-drawn trolley system to carry the politicians to their new quarters. Although a sheet had to be hung to divide the Senate and the House of Representatives, Nevada's legislature could finally meet.

It had been a hectic year for James Nye. He had become governor of the newest and the largest territory in the West, and, by most accounts, he had conducted himself admirably. And Abraham Lincoln would shortly decide to run for re-election and would need James Nye again, this time to make the new Territory of Nevada into a state...

They Called Him Snowshoe

In December, the Sierras are blanketed with snow, and thousands of folks are up there frolicking on the ski slopes. Warmly bundled in $500.00 jumpsuits (donned over thermal underwear) and $300.00 insulated boots, sporting designer sun glasses and swabbed with perfumed protective lotions, they are schussing down machine-groomed trails on professionally engineered, waxed skis. Watching the endless trail of vehicles snaking up the mountainside, it's hard to imagine that scarcely more than 100 years ago there was only one man in either California or Nevada who knew how to ski at all.

John A. Thompson was his name. A lanky Norwegian, he had arrived in Hangtown, today's Placerville, in 1851. For a time, he tried his hand in the California diggings, places like Kelsey's and Coon Hollow, but his luck was hardly more than mediocre.

When winter began to blanket the region, work came to a standstill. Worse yet, communication of any kind was virtually cut off. It was impossible for stagecoaches to traverse the towering Sierra which separated Nevada and California; even lone riders could not get through. The few men who dared attempt a winter crossing on foot, if they survived at all, were usually not in the mood to turn right around to try it again. Angrily, the men grumbled about their mail to postal authorities. They grumbled to the government. They grumbled among themselves. John Thompson offered to do something about it.

He approached postal officials with a proposition: "Give me a chance to carry the mail. If I don't make good, don't pay me. If I do, pay me $200.00 a month." Having nothing to lose, skeptical authorities quickly agreed. They would let him try it as an experiment. That experiment would continue for more than twenty years.

He fashioned skis by splitting oak staves in the manner popular in his native Norway. Each was ten feet long, three inches

45

thick beneath the toe strap, and each weighed an incredible twenty-five pounds. The fittings were nothing more than a couple of cleats lashed against his heels and secured across his toes.

The distance from Hangtown to Carson City was only ninety miles as the crow flies, but it was ninety miles of solid mountain. There were no trails, no rest stops, not even a cabin along the way. Most of the time the wind raged relentlessly, blinding sight, obliterating passageways and natural landmarks. Each new blizzard would completely change the lay of the land. Snowblindness was a constant companion.

On his back he carried a mail pouch that at times weighed as much as 100 pounds. He carried no compass; he didn't need it. On early trips he carried a revolver but later discarded it because of the weight. More amazing still, he never wore an overcoat or even carried a blanket. "Too heavy," he would say. He knew nothing of using wax to keep the snow from sticking to his skis. When they became clogged, he would wait for nightfall when the snow froze again, then ski on in pitch darkness to make up for lost time. When he rested, it would be in the crevice of a rock or beneath a dead tree set afire for warmth. The journey east into Nevada was the hardest. It was also the steepest, requiring three full days and nights as opposed to two for the return trip from Carson City. He used no ski poles, preferring instead a long hardwood staff to steady himself and to use as a brake.

Such was his lonely journey for more than twenty years. From time to time, he would come upon the body of a man frozen in the drifts, a petrified face barely visible among the rocky crags. He would shoulder the corpse and carry it down the mountainside for burial.

Some he came across were luckier. One night Thompson stumbled upon Jim Siston, a pack train operator who had been stranded in the pass. Removing the man's boots, he discovered that frostbite and gangrene had set in. Building the stricken man a fire, he set out immediately for help. He skied on to Carson City all that night. The next morning, he roused five men from bed and returned to the desperate Siston with a sled. Then, it was back down the mountain once again.

In the office of Doctor Dagget, it was determined that immediate amputation of Siston's leg was necessary. But the doctor had no chloroform. In fact, there was no chloroform in all of Carson City. Again, it was up to Thompson.

"I'll get you the chloroform," he said, and, still without sleep, he began yet another trip up into the blizzard. Arriving in Placerville, he learned that the nearest medicine was still far from reach, in Sacramento. When it finally arrived, Thompson lugged it immediately back across the Sierra. That daring episode was written up in newspapers from coast to coast. Snowshoe Thompson became a living legend.

Perhaps the most incredible chapter of his story never truly came to light. In the two decades that he made his daring journey over some of the most treacherous terrain in the country, Snowshoe Thompson was never paid. Each year he would bill the government for services rendered. Each year he received nothing more than a promise. State officials in both Nevada and California eventually petitioned the Federal Government, but, incredibly, the debt was never paid.

On May 15, 1876, Snowshoe Thompson, the living legend, passed on. His wife paid for a tombstone that to this day marks his grave in Genoa, Nevada's first permanent settlement. Atop the simple marker is a small pair of skis carved in stone. They are all that remains of the man who carried the mail through Nevada's winters -- for free.

Joe Goodman: Enterprising Editor

"There has never been a paper like the *Enterprise* on the Coast since and never can be again -- never one so entirely human, so completely the reflex of a splendid personality and a mining camp's buoyant life."

Others have since echoed Wells Drury's appraisal of the *Territorial Enterprise*, Nevada's premier daily during the days of the fabulous Comstock Lode. But frontier newspapers, particularly those that tied themselves precariously to mining, came and went with alarming frequency in the early days of the Silver State. How then did the *Enterprise* become such a spectacular success, a newspaper that truly became a legend?

The *Enterprise* was a newspaper in the right place at the right time; it had fiery editors like forthright Rollin Daggett; it employed a veritable stable of talented, satirical, entertaining writers like Dan DeQuille and Mark Twain. Still, the *Enterprise* would never have become Nevada's premier publication without the dynamic leadership of its young editor, twenty-three-year-old Joe Goodman, a man who, until that time, had never run a newspaper in his life. "He had never operated a business and he had little money," wrote historian George Williams III, "but Goodman was a versatile writer, able to knock out a stream of poetry as easily as prose; he was intelligent and had a clear vision of what a newspaper should be. And, he was willing to take a risk."

And he did. In 1861, Goodman, almost broke, arrived in Virginia City with a young partner, twenty-year-old Dennis McCarthy, in tow. At the time, Virginia City was the biggest and most exciting mining camp in the entire west. Goodman and McCarthy realized immediately that a strong local newspaper, which could provide the essential mix of local mining and regional news, was imperative. As luck would have it, one local paper, established just a short time before by Jonathan Williams, was already on the rocks. Goodman and McCarthy were gutsy if nothing else. Within days the young men had persuaded Williams to sell out for the measly sum of $1,000. The two put up their entire savings -- all forty dollars of it -- as evidence of their good faith. Within a week the *Enterprise* had a new editor, Joe Goodman; McCarthy took over the pressroom.

Goodman's feel for life in Virginia City proved uncannily astute. Within months the struggling newspaper had hundreds of new subscribers, enough to guarantee at least a portion of the operating expenses. Goodman, who recognized that he was no financial genius, wisely turned that aspect of the business over to Jerry Driscoll, who kept a watchful eye on the purse strings.

Mine owners bought huge amounts of advertising space, but Goodman realized that it would be subscriptions purchased by the miners themselves, not advertising, that would prove to be the backbone of a successful future. Where other editors of Comstock papers had kowtowed to the mining interests, under Goodman the *Enterprise* took quite the opposite approach. No mine or banking interest was sacred, a stance that endeared Goodman's paper to the populace and made him a local hero. Subscriptions rose dramatically.

Even the venerable William Sharon, the most powerful banker in the territory, was not immune to the barbs thrown by Goodman's pen. Sharon, hired by William Ralston to manage the Bank of California's Virginia City branch, generously loaned thousands of dollars to the struggling Comstock mine owners. When these monies were gone, spent on mining exploration, new equipment, and wages, the companies turned to Sharon again. "But now," according to George Williams, "Sharon was a different man, cold, calculating, merciless. He would loan no more money. As mining company after mining company defaulted on their loans, Sharon acquired control of Comstock mines and mills. Sharon then invested large sums in the mines and soon became very successful. But it made William Sharon the most despised man in Virginia City."

Joe Goodman was there to lead the attack. When Sharon returned to the Comstock in an attempt to gain backing for a run at the United States Senate, Goodman himself wrote the scathing editorial that greeted him: "Your unexpected return, Mr. Sharon, has afforded no opportunity for public preparation, and you will consequently accept these simple remarks as an unworthy but earnest expression of the sentiments of a people who feel they would be lacking in duty and self-respect if they failed upon such an occasion to make a deserved recognition of your acts and character. You are probably aware that you have returned to a community where you are feared, hated and despised."

But Goodman wasn't through yet. He was about to make this edition of the *Enterprise* the most popular in Virginia City's history. He continued, "Your character in Nevada for the past nine years has been one of merciless rapacity. You fastened yourself upon the vitals of the State like a hyena, and woe to him who disputed with you a single morsel of your prey....You cast honor, honesty, and the commonest civilities aside. You broke faith with men whenever you could subserve your purpose by doing so...."

The editorial, which today would be considered grounds for libel, did the trick. Thanks in part to Goodman's "tell-it-like-it-is" editorial policy, Sharon was defeated in his bid for the prestigious Senate seat in 1872. Only after he managed to purchase the paper himself in 1874, in order to stifle Goodman's loud and boisterous comments, was Sharon able to obtain the position of dignity he coveted so dearly.

Joe Goodman made a fortune from the *Enterprise*. It is said that during the newspaper's glory years, it was making as much as $1,000 a day, at a time when twenty dollars a week was considered extraordinary wages. Historians have written that Goodman actually carried his receipts to the bank in buckets.

When Goodman eventually sold the thriving *Enterprise* to his nemesis, William Sharon, he retired to San Francisco where he invested heavily in the same mining stocks he had been so leery of while in Virginia City. He promptly lost the fortune he had so painstakingly amassed. He then published the *San Francisco*, a weekly, but it eventually went broke. He spent his declining years studying archeology in South America. Still, he had accomplished what he had set out to do. He had made the *Territorial Enterprise* one of the most famous and lucrative newspapers in the west. In the process, he provided an opportunity for growth for a fledgling reporter who was now calling himself Mark Twain.

Though he died in relative obscurity, with little of his fortune, save old issues, to remind him of his impact, Joe Goodman had made the *Territorial Enterprise* a legend in its own time.

Mark One up for Me!

"A lady at the hotel told me to drink a quart of whiskey every 24 hours, and a friend up town recommended precisely the same course. Each advised me to take a quart; that made a half gallon. I did it, and still live!"

A half gallon of whiskey? You bet. Mark Twain, America's favorite writer, was also one of Nevada's most famous drinkers. And therein lies a tale...

American folklore claims that young writer Sam Clemens took the pen name "Mark Twain" from his riverboating days on the Mississippi, the theory being that "mark twain" was the cry of riverboat captains, a term for measuring depth. He first used the pen name in a dispatch from Carson City dated January 31, 1863, and for years scholars have considered the riverboat theory a plausible explanation. But there are those in Nevada who claim that Sam Clemens came by the name for other reasons, most particularly, his penchant for the bottle.

In later years, after his marriage to Olivia Langdon, Twain swore off serious drinking, but during his days on the fabulous Comstock, imbibing was his favorite pastime, and it was legendary in its proportions. His favorite watering holes were the corner bar in Piper's Opera House, the Sazerac on C Street, the Delta, and the International Hotel, where he was known to stand "tall at the bar" until the "wee small hours of the morning." So well-known were his intemperate habits that the Reverend Horatio Stebbins of San Francisco, writing in response to an inquiry from Twain's future father-in-law, predicted that the writer would "fill a drunkard's grave." On his arrival in Virginia City, even Twain himself admitted, "This new mining town, with its romantic name, is one of the best populated and most promising camps, but as to the mines, I have started out several times to inspect them, but never got past the brewery."

Twain's drinking habits, like those of the vast majority of men in the booming mining camp, were well-known. Often he would partake in the company of his closest friends, Dan DeQuille, Rollin Daggett, Dennis McCarthy from the *Territorial Enterprise*, and Steve Gillis, a prospector from Twain's earlier mining days. So regular were their sessions that these men formed a group called "Companions of the Jug," a drinking club whose name was later changed to "the Visigoths" when it was feared that tee-totalling readers of the *Enterprise* might object. The Visigoths held forth nightly in a beer bar conveniently located in the basement of the *Enterprise* building, and, according to Rollin Daggett, their daily consumption was "a ten gallon keg, which was always consumed before the paper went to press."

"Mark was among the regular attendants," wrote Daggett, "and consumed his portion of the daily allowance with the most astonishing regularity, although he seldom indulged in anything more intoxicating than beer."

Still, a ten-gallon keg, even split five ways, is by no means a small amount...

Alf Doten, a reporter famous for his journals about life on the Comstock, concurs. He tells of a trip to the mining camp of Como, east of Carson City, where Mark was apparently more interested in breweries than in mining: "Mark, you don't seem to get out among the mines and write 'em up. If you'll come along with me to the top of the hill I'll point you out all the quartz ledges in the district, give you the names of the mines and the aggravating particulars, just as good as if you tramped all around among them yourself. Splendid view, Mark; come along up and I'll give you the whole thing."

But, according to Doten, Twain had other things on his mind. He replied, "Say, Alf, do you know what you remind me of? You remind me of the fellow we read of in the Bible, called the devil, who took the Savior up on top of a high mountain, where he could see all over the world and offered to give him the whole thing if he would fall down and worship him. Only you ain't the devil and I ain't the Savior, by a blamed sight. How far do you say it is up there? Only half a mile? Well, no, thank you all the same, but I'm too derned lazy. Let's go down to the brewery."

But what does Twain's drinking have to do with how he came by the name Mark Twain? George Cassidy, a writer who knew Twain during Virginia City's glory days, claims that the name originated in Twain's favorite drinking establishment, the Opera House owned by John Piper. Cassidy explains:

We knew Clemens in the early days and know

54

exactly how he became dubbed 'Mark Twain'. John Piper's saloon on B Street used to be the grand rendevous [sic] for all Virginia City Bohemians. Piper conducted a cash business and refused to keep any books. As a special favor, however, he would occasionally chalk down drinks for the boys on the wall back of the bar. Sam Clemens, when localizing for the *Enterprise*, always had an account, with the balance against him on Piper's wall. Clemens was by no means a Coal Oil Tommy -- he drank for the pure and unadulterated love of the ardent. Most of his drinking was conducted in single-handed contests, but occasionally he would invite Dan DeQuille, Charlie Parker, Bob Lowery, or Alf Doten (never more than one of them, however, at a time), and whenever he did, his invariable parting injunction to Piper was to 'Mark Twain', meaning two chalk marks, of course.

Mark Twain got his name from chalk marks on a blackboard? America's most famous writer took his pen name from a bar tab? Say it isn't so! It just seems too far-fetched to be true.

Still, Twain biographer George Williams III seems to agree: "It is easy to imagine Sam Clemens in the Virginia City saloons, his language still full of the river jargon he had used daily for four and a half years, asking the barkeep to 'mark twain' -- place two drinks on his tab. Fellow reporters quickly picked up on this expression and nicknamed Clemens, 'Mark Twain.' Friends were calling Twain 'Mark' before Clemens signed the name to his January 31 dispatch."

Did Mark Twain take his pen name from his early days on the Mississippi, or did others peg him with the colorful moniker? The mystery remains to this day.

Nevada's First Sheriff

He stood six feet two, a lean man, all muscle. He had been a scalphunter, a Texas Ranger, a prospector, and a prison guard before he came to Nevada. And by the time he took up ranching in the sprawling Carson Valley, he was just getting warmed up. His name was Bill Byrnes.

He had come to the valley in a roundabout way. At the age of twenty-two he formed a brief partnership with three men: Jim Beckworth, the famous scout, Jim Lansing, who had been a pirate with John Lafitte, and Bob Carson, brother of the famous Kit Carson. Their purpose: to collect the fifty dollar bounty offered by the Mexican government for scalps of Apache Indians. Their first expedition into Mexico proved to be a successful one, but Byrnes had little stomach for a trade which murdered for a living. To the rescue came the Mexican War; Byrnes promptly joined up.

At war's end, he wandered north to the gold fields of California. En route, he paused briefly in Monterey to get married, but by the time he turned his attention once again to prospecting, most of the gold had already petered out. So Byrnes signed on as a guard at a newly constructed prison in the small village of San Quentin. Within a few months he was promoted to captain of the guards. But after two years at the prison, Brynes headed east once again, this time to Nevada and the sprawling Carson Valley. It was the summer of 1851.

At the time, there was no law in the region. Isolated ranchers and farmers petitioned the federal government for assistance but to no avail. But in November of that year, the citizens formed a government of their own, such as it was. What happened next is still unclear, but suddenly the wandering Bill Byrnes had become the region's first peace officer. Some say that he was duly elected to the post, but no records of an election of any kind exist to this day. Some claim that Byrnes simply stood up at the meeting and was handed a badge.

Either way, Bill Byrnes was the first lawman in the Nevada Territory.

From the start, Byrnes was either loved or hated. He ruled the area with an iron fist and was never loath to use his sidearms. There were numerous complaints about the rough tactics of the new lawman.

N.R. Haskell was a case in point. Haskell, who ran a small trading post located at the mouth of Gold Canyon, was known to harbor a grudge against the new sheriff. One afternoon, Haskell and a companion, Wash Loomis, invited Byrnes to stop by, ostensibly to enjoy some target practice together. After Byrnes had emptied his sixgun at a target, Haskell fired several shots into Byrnes. Hit in the stomach at point blank range, Byrnes slumped to the ground. Haskell and Loomis did not wait around for a hangman; they quickly packed some supplies and left the Territory.

But Byrnes survived, and within six weeks he was back on the job. But now *he* held a grudge; no one could shoot the sheriff in broad daylight and get away with it, he reasoned. Soon, Byrnes was taking lengthy "hunting" trips out of the area. Locals wondered aloud what kind of "game" he was hunting. After several months Byrnes returned from one of his trips and announced that his "hunting" days were over. He refused to offer any further information, but folks noted that Haskell and Loomis were never seen or heard from again.

Bill Byrnes would soon leave Nevada. After little more than a year as Nevada's first sheriff, he decided he had had enough. Town fathers had been wondering openly whether Byrnes should be asked to resign. Citizens who, just months before, had been pleading for any kind of law and order, now questioned their decision in whispered conversation.

But it would not be disgruntled citizenry that would drive Bill Byrnes from his job. He had other things on his mind, namely his health. Years of roaming the west, fighting Indians side-by-side with famous scouts, battling Mexican troops and American outlaws, had taken its toll.

When he checked into a San Francisco hospital, doctors were shocked at what they found. Bill Byrnes had a total of thirty-two bullet wounds in his body! Several bullets were still lodged dangerously near his heart. Immediately they ordered an operation.

Those were the days before anesthesia. To help ease the pain of the surgery, Byrnes was strapped down and given whiskey. Before he passed out, his screams could be heard throughout the hospital as the doctors cut into his chest. They found three old bullets lodged dangerously near his heart; further examination revealed another bullet lodged in his skull. The doctors did what they could and closed him up. Though still in considerable pain, Byrnes left the hospital against doctor's orders in the spring of 1853.

He didn't have long to wait for a new adventure...

At the time, California was plagued by a string of daring hold-ups orchestrated by a Mexican bandit known as Joaquin Murietta. In May of 1853, so notorious had the outlaw become that the California State Assembly passed a resolution to organize a company of men to be known as the California Rangers. Governor Bigler appointed a fellow named Harry Love to head the mounted posse. It wasn't long before Bill Byrnes, though still ailing, signed up.

For months, Love and his Rangers tracked the elusive Murietta. Other holdups, attributed erroneously to the outlaw, led the men far afield for many weeks. Finally, they found the bandit's camp just south of Los Angeles.

As the Rangers rushed the encampment, Murietta recognized Byrnes. He mounted his horse and charged. Byrnes fired two shots, and the outlaw slumped to the ground. Bill Byrnes' daughter recounted what happened next. As the ex-sheriff approached the outlaw, Murietta rose up. Quickly Byrnes leveled his pistol for a final shot. "Don't shoot me, Bill. I'm dead," pleaded the bandit. With that, he gasped and died. It was July 3, 1853.

As proof of their mission's success and to dispel any attempt to martyr the outlaw, the head of Joaquin Murietta was severed from his body and taken by the Rangers to headquarters. For a time it was on display in San Francisco until, during the famous earthquake of 1906, it tumbled from a shelf and was lost forever.

After his encounter with Murietta, information about Bill Byrnes remains sketchy. He did return to the Carson Valley, just in time to charge into another conflict. Within a few weeks, an Indian uprising, which became known as the Paiute Indian Wars, erupted. Byrnes enlisted as a volunteer and rode off to confront the powerful Chief Winnemucca. Though the encounter has horribly lopsided and could hardly be called a "war" at all, Bill Byrnes received yet another bullet wound for his troubles.

Eventually the pain from his many wounds became increasingly unbearable. To ease the misery, he began drinking whiskey like water, then turned to opium when the whiskey failed. Soon, Byrnes was hopelessly addicted.

In 1870, he was admitted to a Sacramento hospital to take the "cure." But he was too far gone. From Sacramento, he was moved to an asylum for the insane in Stockton, where he remained for almost a decade, unable to recall any of his extraordinary exploits. On June 18, 1883, his mind completely gone, Bill Byrnes died. With him went a part of Nevada history.

Four Men to Be Hung in Half an Hour

Territorial Governor James Nye was worried. The boomtown of Aurora was giving the fledgling Nevada Territory a bad name. Violence was rampant in the town; there had been twenty-seven murders in less than three months. The Governor vowed to put a stop to it and sent a wire to Aurora officials. In it he warned that law and order, at all costs, must be preserved. If Aurora was unable to control the violent nature of its citizenry, asserted the Governor, perhaps the state militia should. But the townsfolk of Aurora had other things on their minds. They fired back a telegram of their own. It said simply: "All quiet and orderly. Four men to be hung in half an hour."

It had begun with a killing. A man by the name of John Rodgers had come upon a horse thief, one Jim Sears. Harsh words turned violent, and Sears was killed. Now under other circumstances, the death of a low-life horse thief would have hardly raised eyebrows in Aurora. But Sears had been a member of the Dailey gang, a band of vicious cutthroats that had been terrorizing Aurora for months. John Dailey vowed revenge on the man who had shot a member of his gang and, incidentally, anyone else who might have been involved.

It was nearing nightfall when the Dailey gang rode up to the stage stop operated by Billy Johnson, a friend of Rodgers. Johnson was a likeable fellow who ran the station full time and cultivated potatoes on the side. "Where's Rodgers?" demanded Dailey. Johnson refused to divulge the whereabouts of his friend. Dailey was about to pull his gun when several passengers appeared on the steps of the station. Not wanting to threaten the old man in front of witnesses, Dailey wheeled his horse, and he and his gang rode off. From that day on both Rodgers and Johnson were living on borrowed time.

The following week, Billy Johnson loaded his wagon with potatoes and prepared to leave on the long journey to Aurora. Friends advised him not to go, fearing that members of the Dailey gang would

61

waylay him en route, but Johnson simply shrugged and drove off. His trip to Aurora was uneventful. Night was falling by the time he unloaded his wagon and he decided to stay in town. He stabled his team and reserved a fifty-cent bed. Then he retired to a saloon for a little libation.

The townsfolk could not recall exactly what happened next. They did remember that a stranger had bellied up to the bar beside Billy Johnson, and the two had engaged in a lengthy conversation. The next minute, however, they were gone. No one was sure if the two men had left together.

When the door of the saloon flew open and John Dailey strode in, no one thought much of it. But then he made his way to the bar, ordered a drink, and, as he raised his glass to his lips, casually remarked that there was a dead man out in the alley. Momentarily all eyes were upon him; then the men in the bar rushed outside.

The body of Billy Johnson was hardly recognizable. He had been severely beaten; his throat had been slashed from ear to ear so deeply that his head was almost completely severed. Coal oil had been poured on his body and ignited. As if to add insult to injury, his body had also been peppered with bullets. John Dailey had disappeared.

A posse was formed; Sheriff B.J. Francis led the men in quick pursuit. They managed to overtake Dailey and two members of his gang, Jim Masterson and Three-Fingered Jack, in an arroyo to the west of town. A fourth member of the gang, Bill Buckley, managed to escape.

The capture of the Dailey gang was on everyone's lips. They would be brought to trial, of course, but few of Aurora's honest citizens actually believed that the men would be convicted. Fear of the Dailey gang had intimidated juries in the past.

It was then that someone had an idea. If a jury wouldn't convict Dailey, perhaps it was time for the townsfolk to take the law into their own hands...

A meeting was held in the Wingate Building. Surprisingly enough, more than 350 citizens showed up. They formed themselves into a group called the Citizen's Safety Committee, appointed J.A. Palmer their official peace officer, and promptly declared marshal law. From then on, they decided, the streets of Aurora would be closed by nine o'clock. To emphasize their determination, the group raided the armory of the local militia, confiscated the guns, and distributed them to Committee members who began patrolling the streets. Never had it been so quiet in the boomtown of Aurora.

With the town firmly under control, members of the Safety Committee rode off in pursuit of the remaining outlaw, Bill Buckley.

They had ridden about half a day when they were met by Sheriff Francis and his posse returning with Buckley in tow. The committee took Buckley into custody, and, for good measure, arrested Francis as well, thereby relieving him of further responsibilities.

On February 9, 1864, nine days after Billy Johnson had been murdered, Dailey, Three-Fingered Jack, Masterson, and Buckley were hoisted upon a crude scaffold on the outskirts of town. Dailey and Buckley openly admitted to the killing of Billy Johnson; Three-Fingered Jack and Masterson swore they had nothing to do with it and pleaded for their lives. Their cries fell on deaf ears. Hoods were placed over their heads, and with the entire town watching, the four men dropped through the trap doors and into eternity.

When Governor James Nye completed his telegram to Aurora demanding law and order, little did he know that it had already arrived.

It Was Just a Sack of Flour

In 1864, tempers were flaring in the boomtown of Austin. Only two years before the town had sprung to life when news of the discovery of a rich outcropping of ore swept across the Nevada Territory. Although Austin was isolated, located in the exact geographic center of what would soon become the state of Nevada, almost overnight men swarmed like locusts into the region with hopes of getting in on a piece of the action. Along with their hopes and dreams, the miners brought with them their sympathies as well.

The American Civil War had been raging for years. Unlike the miners in Virginia City, who were predominantly pro-Union, Northern and Southern men were almost equally divided in the new camp. That made the living a mite uneasy. The only recreation in the boomtown was drinking, and fistfights over the outcome of the war were common. More than one resident of the newly created Boot Hill had argued unsuccessfully for his cause.

But some of the confrontations were friendly. Take the case of Reuel Colt Gridley, a businessman, and H.S. Herrick, a local doctor. Gridley was a staunch Democrat; Herrick was a Republican, and therein lies a tale.

It was the mayor's race which started it all. Gridley favored a Democratic candidate, Mr. Buel. Herrick spoke out against Buel in no uncertain terms. Learning of the disparaging remarks being made against his candidate, Gridley confronted Herrick on the main street of the town with a friendly bet: "Herrick, I'll stake a wager with you. I say that Buel will be elected Mayor. If he be elected, you will carry a fifty-pound sack of flour from Clifton to upper Austin to the tune of 'Dixie.' If he be defeated, I shall carry the flour over the same course to the tune of 'Old John Brown.'"

Before long the entire town of Austin knew of the wager. Regardless of the outcome, it would be no mean feat. The terrain between Clifton and Austin was treacherous at best, even without a fifty-pound sack of flour. It was uphill all the way. Side money flowed freely as the people of Austin anxiously awaited the outcome of the election. Buel lost.

On April 20th, preceded by musicians, city officials, thirty-six men on horseback, and Dr. Herrick, carrying Gridley's hat and cane, Gridley prepared to pay his debt. Gridley's granddaughter described her grandfather, "bearing on his shoulder a sack of flour, which was gaily bedecked with red, white and blue ribbons and flags. He was accompanied by his thirteen-year-old son, Amos. Then came the Democratic City Central Committee, two of whom carried banners; one a huge sponge held aloft on a pole, and another a broomstick. A group of citizens followed and a crowd of boys and Indians brought up the rear." Everyone was prepared to have fun at Gridley's expense: "As the cortege passed by the spectators cheered, whistles were blown, and good feeling prevailed generally. The band played 'Old John Brown' and the bystanders took up the chorus and sang 'Glory, Glory, Hallelujah'...."

When Gridley's bet was paid, the huge throng retired to the local saloon, presumably, wrote Gridley's granddaughter, "for the sole purpose of deciding the fate of the flour." Suggestions, liberally laced with ample supplies of whiskey, flowed. Republicans in the group felt that the Democrats should be forced to make pancakes for them. But Gridley had other ideas: "This crowd of people has had its fun at my expense. Now let us see who will do the most for our sick and wounded soldiers. We will put this flour up and auction it off, with the understanding that it belongs to the bidder only until such time as another bid is made for it. The proceeds will go to the Sanitary Commission."

Gridley's suggestion was apt for those feeling guilty about leaving the battlefield in search of fame and fortune. The Sanitary Commission was a Civil War nursing organization, the forerunner of the American Red Cross. A youngster was sent off running to bring the town's only auctioneer, T.B. Wade. Gridley himself made the first bid, the sizeable sum of $300.

Within the next few hours, Gridley's sack of flour was sold again and again. By the time the sun set, over $4,000 had been raised to treat the veterans of the far away battlefields. Reuel Gridley had paid off his bet in spades.

But the story doesn't end there. Rumors of Gridley's auction spread like wildfire throughout the state. Within hours it reached Nevada's largest town, Virginia City, where the story came to the attention of Mark Twain at the *Territorial Enterprise,* who recognized

Gridley's name as that of an old boyhood friend from Hannibal, Missouri. He wired Gridley right away: "Fetch along your flour sack!"

Twain, a Southerner, set up a meeting with Gridley and another Virginia City businessman, Northerner Almarin Paul. The three men reasoned that perhaps they could capitalize on the patriotism generated in Austin, stage a fund-raiser in Virginia City as well, and mend the rift between Northern and Southern sympathizers while having fun at the same time. So another auction was held.

Despite their high hopes, the group's first attempt was disappointing. Thousands of miners were expected, and it was hoped that $20,000 could be raised. After all, wasn't Virginia City the Queen of the Comstock and the richest city of them all? Unfortunately, only a few hundred men showed up; the pot totalled a mere $580.

Feeling dejected, the three retired to the *Enterprise* to think things over. That meeting would result in one of the largest and most successful fund-raising campaigns in Nevada history, ingeniously simple in its execution. The men theorized that, if they could not shame the miners into donating by appealing to their patriotism, perhaps they could stir their ardor by concentrating on their civic pride and the constant rivalry among the silver camps of the Comstock Lode.

After the disappointing results of the Virginia City auction, Gridley, Twain, and Paul regrouped and devised a new scheme. Reuel Gridley took his flour sack on a grand tour of the Nevada mining camps, and soon news of the fabulous wager spread throughout the boomtowns of Nevada.

Author Elbert Edwards picks up the story: "The following morning the trio rode out of Virginia City toward Gold Hill in a procession of patriotically decorated carriages, preceded by a brass band playing patriotic tunes. As they proceeded, they picked up a following that constituted a fair parade. There, the sack of flour was auctioned off repeatedly in the same manner as in Austin."

The fanfare paid off. The miners of Gold Hill paid over $6,000 for Gridley's sack of flour, considerably more than had been raised in Austin. Twain, Paul, and Gridley proceeded on to Silver City, then Dayton. At both towns the miners contributed far more than those in Virginia City. Now Twain and his Virginia City cohorts were truly embarrassed. Twain immediately sent dispatches to the *Enterprise*, emphasizing the fact that the miners of Gold Hill, Silver City, and Dayton were "far more generous" than those of his own hometown.

His press release had the desired effect. "Bring back that sack of flour!" wired the Virginia City miners. By the following day, when the trio returned to Virginia City, miners from all along the Divide had gathered to defend the reputation of their town. This time Virginia

City was taking no chances in coming in second best to a bunch of upstart mining camps. Twain initiated an open challenge between his newspaper, the *Enterprise*, and its rival, the *Union*. The townsfolk eagerly awaited the arrival of the flour sack. A giant parade was staged through the streets of the city, which resounded with music from a score of brass bands. Store fronts were decorated with torch lights and American flags. So effective was the advance publicity that the procession, which had begun as a mere trickle, spread out in a line more than a mile long. Mark Twain magnanimously dubbed it "The Army of the Lord."

By this time, Gridley was no longer walking. He and his now-famous flour sack rode comfortably next to Twain and Paul in an expensive open carriage decorated with colorful bunting. As they passed the cheering throng, gold coins, tattered money pouches, mining shares, and even firearms began flying through the air. The response was overwhelming. Mining companies ponied up as did wealthy prostitutes and poor Chinese. Even the beggars of Virginia City, the Paiutes, got into the act. All day long, the men bid and then re-bid for Gridley's now dog-eared flour sack. When it was all over, the carriage was loaded down with donations. When the dust had finally settled, over $14,000 had been raised for the Sanitary Commission. The miners of Nevada had ponied up over $25,000 for the disabled soldiers of the Civil War.

The next problem was getting the money to the New York headquarters of the Commission. After considerable thought, it was decided to send a true emblem of Nevada's wealth and support, a gift so unique that it would be sure to attract attention and convince easterners that silver-seekers were doing more than shirking their duty and escaping the horrors of the war. The mining stocks were sold, coins were exchanged, and chunks of ore were melted down. Wrote Edwards, "This money collected on the Comstock was reduced to silver bars and shipped to the president of the United States Sanitary Commission in New York City. The eight silver bars, weighing 7,972 ounces, were carried across the continent cost free by Wells, Fargo and Company." Each bar was engraved with the name of a famous Civil War battle -- Chickamauga, Gettysburg, Vicksburg...

When Dr. Henry Bellows, the president of the National Sanitary Commission, received the extraordinary delivery, he called a special meeting. As it was nearing Christmas, it was decided to hold a special get-together in a local theater. Bellows promised a special treat for his guests, and the place was filled to overflowing. The good doctor did not disappoint them.

Just at the guests had settled back in their seats, a band

struck up "The Star Spangled Banner." The curtain slowly rose, and there on the stage was a giant Christmas tree; from its branches hung the bars of silver from Virginia City. The donation was the largest sum ever received at one time by the Sanitary Commission, and those bars would go down in American history as the most expensive decorations ever to adorn even the most magnificent of Christmas trees. Both records brought glowing newspaper accounts of the patriotism that abounded in that far-off wilderness of Nevada.

But that's not the end of the story, for Gridley still was not content. On the other side of the Sierra Nevada were other camps teeming with miners equally patriotic. As Gridley boarded a stagecoach for the California gold camps, Twain wired ahead, spreading the word of Nevada's great generosity. Californians responded to the challenge. They weren't about to let the miners of Nevada outshine them. Gridley's auction far exceeded even his own wildest expectations. Within the next year, he managed to raise more than $200,000 with his fifty-pound sack of flour. It would go down in history as one of the greatest accomplishments of the war.

Although Mark Twain's little "Army of the Lord" never succeeded in putting an end to the confrontations between Northern and Southern sympathizers on the Comstock, it did succeed in another, perhaps more important task. It managed to prove that silver-crazed Nevadans, so far from the blood of the battlefield, still cared.

And Reuel Gridley, the businessman from Austin, had pulled it off. He had succeeded in raising more money for the Commission than anyone in the entire country. By the time his quest was over, he had accumulated almost a quarter of a million dollars with which to treat the sick and wounded of the War Between the States. But it never would have happened without a race for mayor in the isolated boomtown of Austin.

Thank You, Arizona!

The area that today encompasses the city of Las Vegas, perhaps the most valuable piece of real estate in all of Nevada, was once a part of Arizona. And Arizona certainly didn't take kindly to giving it up.

It was in the late 1850's when the first Mormon settlers filtered into the area and established a mission at Las Vegas. They thrived on farming and mining for several years before being ordered to return to church headquarters in Salt Lake City. Following the Mormon exodus, only a few isolated ranchers populated the area until, in early 1865, a number of settlements began to spring up along the Muddy River. Today, most of them are under water, covered by the building of Boulder Dam, later renamed Hoover Dam, and the creation of Lake Mead. But for a time, St. Thomas, St. Joseph, West Point, Overton, and Callville, all located at the end of the navigable water of the Colorado River, prospered. But the area would soon become embroiled in controversy.

When the Nevada Territory was originally established in 1861, the state's western boundary was loosely defined as following the ridge of the Sierra Nevada mountain range. When a dispute between Nevada and California ensued, the United States Congress, in an attempt to pacify both parties, agreed to take some land on the western border away from Nevada. In compensation, it also decided to give the Silver State more land on the east. As a result, some property was taken from the Utah Territory, and other land to the south was taken from Arizona.

The amount of land in question was considerable, more than 12,000 square miles, encompassing what today is Clark County. Utah hardly complained. After all, Mormon allegiance to Salt Lake City was stronger than any political ties to either Nevada or Arizona. But Arizona officials weren't so understanding. They refused to recognize the government grant. There was trouble brewing on the horizon.

The settlers along the Muddy River were surprised when one day some Arizona officials arrived. Wrote Thomas Smith, Presiding Elder of the Muddy Valley settlements, "Some politicians had made a visit to St. Thomas and St. Joseph on an electioneering tour. They were from Fort Mohave and claimed that the Muddy Settlements were in Arizona and that elections would be held on Tuesday, 5th of September...."

The settlements were still part of Arizona? The news was startling to Elder Smith. Even more shocking was the fact that the Arizona delegates revealed that Mohave County, in which most of the Muddy settlements were located, would be divided to add Pah-Ute County. The delegates from Arizona sternly suggested that individuals should be elected to represent their towns in the Arizona Territory legislature. In the interim, they appointed Smith their assessor and tax collector.

The Territory of Arizona was rightfully concerned. After all, the region in question contained most of the navigable portions of the Colorado River, the lifeblood of the area. On November 5, 1866, Arizona's legislature drafted a letter to the Senate and the House of Representatives. "[This region] holds a natural and convenient relation to the Territory of Arizona, and a most unnatural and inconvenient one to the State of Nevada," wrote Arizona's delegation. "It is the water shed of the Colorado River into which all the principal streams of Arizona empty....By this great river the Territory receives most of its supplies, and lately it has become the channel of a large part of the trade of San Francisco with Utah and Montana." The letter went on to point out that the region was vital to convenient shipping in the area: "While it is a comparatively short and easy journey from any part of the territory in question to the county seats or capital of Arizona, it is a tedious and perilous one of 300 miles to the nearest county seat in Nevada and to reach the capital of that state, by reason of intervening deserts including the celebrated 'Death Valley', over which travel is often impossible and always extremely hazardous, it is necessary to go around by Los Angeles and San Francisco, a distance of some 1500 miles."

Arizona summed up its position in no uncertain terms: "It is the unanimous wish of the inhabitants of Pah-Ute and Mohave Counties, and indeed of all constituents of your memorialists, that the territory in question should remain in Arizona."

But Congress failed to respond; Nevada's authorization to absorb that northwestern portion of Arizona was never repealed. Nevada Governor Henry Blasdel wasted no time in taking the matter before the state legislature. Wrote Blasdel, "This grant, connecting us as it does with the navigable waters of the Colorado River, and embracing extensive and valuable agricultural and mineral lands, is of great importance to the State and should be promptly accepted."

It was. Blasdel went on to suggest a vote of the people to ratify the constitution, "conforming our southern boundary to the line designated in the grant." But the legislature, content perhaps with the old adage that says that possession is nine-tenths of the law, simply pushed the matter aside. Not until 1981 was a measure approved by the Nevada legislature to conform the constitutional boundary of the Silver State to its actual boundary; that measure was ratified by the voters in 1982.

All the property south of the 37th parallel had, overnight, been added to Nevada's territory, and the state, already one of the largest in the country, had suddenly become even larger. The Congress of the United States had robbed Peter to pay Paul.

Realizing that the area today is Clark County and contains Las Vegas, Nevada's largest city, Nevadans should be mighty glad they did.

Builders of the West

They worked with simple tools -- picks, shovels, and chisels. They lived on a sparse diet of oysters, dried fish, sweet rice crackers, bamboo shoots, and seaweed; on holidays there was a little pork. They worked with sheer determination, stamina, and guts, little more. And together they accomplished a task that few thought could ever be done; together they completed the most difficult portion of a railroad line that ran across the entire country. Their amazing accomplishment would rival the building of the Great Pyramids of Egypt.

The winter of 1866 was the kind that had doomed the Donner Party. But the unrelenting snows were of secondary concern to Charles Crocker. Crocker, one of the infamous Big Four that included Collis Huntington, Mark Hopkins, and Leland Stanford, the newly elected Governor of California, was in a race against time. The Railroad Act of 1862, authorizing a railroad west from Omaha, Nebraska, to the Pacific, had been signed by President Lincoln in 1864, and a group of eastern financiers had already begun the westward construction of the Union Pacific line. Crocker was determined to head east at an incredible pace, laying over 1,000 miles of track in the process.

The task was a formidable one. Before him were the Sierra Nevada mountains, an chain of solid granite where the lowest pass rose more than 7,000 feet, where winter snows blanketed the region with forty foot depths. The path would have to rise at the unheard of rate of 140 feet to the mile, and the treacherous gorges of the Sierra would have to be filled by tons of earth. Even if the mountains could somehow be tamed, the desolation of Nevada still lay beyond, a parched expanse with no food or water for hundreds of miles. Could it be done? That was the question that thousands of Americans, including many in the halls of Congress, were asking.

But the bold Crocker, a giant who tipped the scales at 250 pounds, had a secret weapon. He planned to use Chinese labor. To the scoffers he simply replied, "They built the Great Wall of China, didn't they?"

Crocker recruited more than 15,000 of them in all. They labored endlessly for as long as fourteen hours a day, for wages of as little as twenty-five dollars a month. They fought blizzards so fierce that some of the tiny workers, fresh from the rice paddies of their native China, were swept violently from the slopes of the Sierra, their bodies never recovered. They survived scalding temperatures of more than 120 degrees in the stark and forbidding Nevada desert; yet not a single complaint, spoken or written, has ever survived. In 1863, only eighteen miles of track had been laid east from Sacramento. The following year, that number had dwindled to twelve. But Crocker remained confident. After all, hadn't Congress just allocated $100 million to the project?

"Crocker's Pets," as the Canton Chinese were called, proved to be as industrious as they were uncomplaining. By May of 1866, his Oriental laborers, now numbering close to 15,000, had managed to clear a path for almost 100 miles of track. Crocker himself rode up and down the line on payday, calling the name of each worker in pidgin English, personally handing each man his pay from two saddlebags, one containing silver, the other gold.

Still, the mountains would prove more treacherous than even Crocker had anticipated. Fifteen tunnels had to be drilled through the granite face, and at times the blasting powder did little more than discolor the rock. Some of the workmen toiled completely underground for weeks at a time, picking away at the mountain, inch by inch.

As the laborers neared the summit, avalanches became a constant threat. The men were still struggling with the Sierra by the second, even more disastrous, winter of 1868. Sawmills hastily erected nearby stripped more than sixty-five million board feet of timber from the slopes to build snowsheds that clung precariously to the cliffs. Nevertheless, by June of that year, the summit was breached, and Crocker was able to link up with rails that had already been laid on the eastern side. It had cost the lives of many of his workmen and more than $23 million dollars, but the mountain had been conquered.

But still ahead lay the desert. Here Crocker learned the value of the wide-brimmed coolie hats which other workers had ridiculed. Protected from the searing heat, the Chinese set out to tame yet another forbidding obstacle.

Despite the hardship and slave wages, there was only one instance where the obedient Chinese refused to work. Someone had circulated a rumor that the Nevada desert was home to a giant species of snake, reptiles so large that they could swallow a man whole. So effective was the story that historian Irving Stone reported that more than 1,000 laborers left their jobs and began to walk back to San Francisco before Crocker could convince them that they would be safe. Now confident that the end was in sight, he wired his associates: "After the mountain, we cannot be beaten. Send me the materials I need, and I can build a mile a day of complete railroad."

And he did. On May 10, 1869, dignitaries gathered near five hastily erected saloons in the new town of Promontory, Utah, and Leland Stanford drove the final spike. There were no Chinese in attendance.

The completion of the Transcontinental Railroad would go down in American history as the country's greatest engineering accomplishment. But it never would have happened without the industrious Chinese. So far from home, ridiculed for their dress and manner, the Chinese laborers fought unflinchingly, without complaint, the heavy mountain snows and the choking heat of the summer desert. They were the builders of the west.

Drink 'Til You Drop

The Horse and Mule live thirty years,
Yet know nothing of wines and beers.
Most Goats and Sheep at twenty die,
And have never tasted Scotch or Rye.
A Sow drinks water by the ton,
So at eighteen is mostly done.
The Dog in milk and water soaks,
And then in twelve short years he croaks.
Your modest, sober, bone-dry Hen,
Lays eggs for nogs, then dies at ten.
All animals are strictly dry,
They sinless live, then swiftly die.
But sinful, ginful, beer-soaked men,
Survive three score years and ten.
While some of us, though might few,
Stay sozzled till we're ninety-two!

Whiskey in Nevada -- it came with the territory. There's a certain logic to it: when the sun went down in the majority of tent cities and mining camps that were strewn randomly throughout the desert, there was little left to do but sit and sip. The anonymous poem chronicled by Richard Erdoes in *Saloons of the Old West*, says it all. Whiskey and the early miner were pals.

Although there were literally hundreds of different brands, in general there were only three categories of whiskey offered along the frontier. The first was the "good stuff." Usually it was imported and of top quality, similar to what is available today. But the scarcity of such quality products normally put them far beyond the pocketbooks of itinerant prospectors.

In the second category was the all-purpose bar whiskey, and it was powerful stuff. Wrote Erdoes, "Tongue Oil induced a man to talk his head off, Red Disturbance raised a blood blister on a rawhide boot, and Corpse Reviver made the dead rise." With a touch of humor he noted that Lamp Oil "kept a man well lit," and that a whiskey called Miner's Friend "was advertised to outblast any other explosive."

Bar whiskey packed a whollop all right, though in many cases it was watered down to conform more readily to the saloonkeeper's personal idea of an acceptable profit margin. One such whiskey, known as Old Snakehead, actually had a rattler's head nailed to the inside of the barrel "for flavor." In some of the more isolated saloons, most whiskey was served from unlabeled bottles. The miners, therefore, took to naming the libations with colorful titles of their own. There was Moral 'Suasion, Scamper Juice, Phlegm Cutter, Widow-Maker, Gut Warmer, and Nose Paint. Tonsil Varnish, Stagger Soup, Gas Remover, and Diddle Liquor were there too. This imaginative nomenclature also included the ever-popular Coffin Varnish, Tangle Leg, Nockum Stiff, and the old standby Panther Piss, an atomic concoction which was rumored to contain more than thirty different ingredients.

According to Erdoes, "There was Brigham Young Whiskey -- one jolt and you're a polygamist seeing double, or Dust Cutter for those dry enough to spit cotton. Forty Rods brought a fellow down at exactly that distance, Apache Tears made the roughest customer weep, and Taos Lightning struck a man on the spot." Wedding Whiskey, still being brewed in Swedish villages in North Dakota, was made of "120 proof Everclear Grain Alcohol, burned sugar and crushed peaches. Aphrodisiac herbs were added to 'make the bridegroom go!'"

Unfortunately, a third type of whiskey was also common along the frontier. Although occasionally it could be found in saloons managed by unscrupulous operators, it was brewed primarily for trade with the Indians. It was so potent that a hefty dose could cause blindness -- even death. This recipe from *Saloons of the Old West* attests to the deadly contents:

> One barrel of water
> Two gallons of raw alcohol
> Two ounces of strychnine (to make them crazy)
> Three ounces of tobacco to make them sick (cause Injuns won't believe it's good unless it makes them sick)
> Five bars of soap to give it a bead
> 1/2 pound of red pepper to give it a

kick
Boil with sagebrush until brown.
Strain through a barrel.

Indian whiskey: powerful and deadly. It would become known to whites as "firewater," a result in part of the fact that many Indians would splash a mouthful on an open fire to insure that the drink was not plain old river water.

Of course, Nevada's alcohol was certainly not limited to the confines of the saloon. Limerick's Great Southern Liniment was a favorite of both men and women. Advertised that it was "guaranteed" to cure "Rheumatism, Neuralgia, Ring Worm, Sore Nipples, Chapped Hands, Burns, Bruises, Scalds, Sprains, Cuts, Cancers, Corns, Gout, Broken Breasts, Fever Sores and Inflammation, Sore Eyes, Headaches," and *more*, the liquid was primarily pure alcohol. Even preachers and aging spinsters, those most likely to publicly denounce the evils of drink, were known to carry a bottle of the liniment "for special ailments and special occasions." If Limerick's was unavailable, there was always Dr. E.C. West's Nerve and Brain Treatment -- "Health is Wealth!", Dr. B.J. Kendall's Blackberry Balsam, and Hosteller's Famous Bitters.

Although people are now more aware of its abuses, the role of whiskey hasn't really changed very much since the frontier days. But the names are not as colorful, perhaps because whiskey and the wild west went hand in hand.

The City That Was Washoe

Most travellers taking the short but scenic drive between Reno and Carson City are unaware that there lie the remains of what once was the largest city in the territory. Today nothing is left of the town called Washoe City, save for a few old headstones and a dry lake whose waters rise and fall with the seasons, but at one time there were 5,000 people in residence there.

Those were exciting times. With discovery of silver on the slopes of Mount Davidson, mines were springing up with reckless abandon. Soon the town of Virginia City sprang up as well. To the people of the territory, the future looked good.

But as the mining industry grew, so did the problems of processing the ore. Getting the ore out of the deep, underground mines was one thing, getting the silver out of the ore was quite another. The miners needed almost unlimited supplies of timber to shore up the tunnels. And once the ore was brought to the surface, stamp mills were required to crush the rock. Those mills needed timber as well. To compound the problem, mischievous Mother Nature hadn't helped a bit: her silver and timber were on two different mountain ranges.

The problem was simple, the solution was not. Carrying the ore down from Mount Davidson, then up to the timber supply, was impossible. Carrying the timber directly to the mines was almost as difficult. What was needed was to split the difference, to build a facility somewhere between the two. If ore could be brought down from the eastern mountains, and timber could be brought down from the west, it would be a simple gravity haul for both.

Almost overnight, the town of Washoe sprang up. By 1861, its residents, convinced that the region had an endlessly bright future, were clamoring for the creation of a separate territory. The Territory of Nevada was soon carved from Utah, a county by the name of Washoe was created, and a seat of government was established in the new town of Washoe City. Within a few short years, the town boasted a huge brick courthouse, a new wooden jail, two schools, a newspaper, and a score of bustling businesses.

From the beginning Washoe City was a beehive of activity. Freight wagons rolled along the main street almost twenty-four hours a day. Stamp and lumber mills were working around the clock. Violence, as in the case of many boomtowns, was commonplace.

But the shootout that took place in 1863, was anything but. It involved one of the town's most outstanding citizens, George Derickson, editor of the *Washoe City Times*, the town's first newspaper, and one of his own subscribers, H.F. Swayze.

Swayze had been a source of irritation to the *Times'* young editor for quite some time. On one occasion, Swayze had demanded that the newspaper print an article he had written entitled, "How I Got My Wife," and then provide him with free copies as well. Derickson printed the story but refused to come up with the samples. Swayze stormed out of the newspaper office screaming obscenities at the top of his lungs.

Time did little to assuage Swayze's temper. Several weeks later, he arrived at the office of the *Times* with yet another literary creation. This one, in no uncertain terms, blasted the citizens of Ophir, Washoe City's nearest neighbor. Derickson, not willing to fuel a rivalry between the two towns, refused to publish it.

History is unclear about what happened next. According to an article in the *Virginia City Union*, a loud argument erupted in the newspaper office, followed by gunfire. When the smoke cleared, Swayze staggered, bleeding profusely, into the street. There, blood pouring from his mouth, he spit out a bullet and several of his teeth before collapsing in front of an anxious crowd.

At first, the townspeople thought that Editor Derickson had emerged the victor. But as they cautiously entered the newspaper office, the men found Derickson dead in a pool of blood. Swayze's first bullet had done him in. Swayze was taken into custody on a charge of murder.

Although Swayze claimed that the shooting of Editor Derickson was self defense, few people believed him. Most of the citizens of Washoe City were aware of the long-standing dispute between the editor and contributor, and the majority of them considered Swayze to be irrational and eccentric. A jury convicted him on a charge of manslaughter and sentenced him to the Nevada State Prison for three years.

By the time Swayze was released from prison, the boomtown of Washoe City was already on the decline. By 1868, the ore supply in

Virginia City had dropped dramatically. To make matters worse, a new city, this one called Reno, had started to grow along the new transcontinental railroad line. When Reno petitioned the legislature to move the county seat from Washoe City to Reno, the die was cast.

In 1871, the fine brick courthouse, the pride of Washoe City and the Valley, was dismantled. It was moved, brick by brick, to its new home in Reno. By 1875, fewer than seventy-five people lived in the town that once boasted 5,000. The body of the young editor, George Derickson, had been laid to rest in California; Swayze, discharged from prison, had disappeared. And the town? The bright flame that had once been Washoe City had quietly flickered out.

Epitaph for a Lady

Julia Bulette: everyone knows her story. She ran one of the most expensive houses of prostitution on the frontier; she was Nevada's most famous Lady of the Evening. Unlike most females who had chosen the world's oldest profession, Bulette did not hide her business from the community. Instead, she chose to flaunt it, and in doing so, she became one of Virginia City's leading citizens, one of the most popular folks in town. But, as much as she was loved by some, she was hated by others; there were many who applauded when her body was found.

Bulette had been officially adopted by Virginia City's Engine Company Number One. She was given her own badge and even outfitted with a special uniform. On more than one occasion she appeared, dressed in her "official" uniform, to lend a hand during an emergency. There was a popular joke in the city that she would spring from bed to answer any fire summons, not just those belonging to Company Number One. No matter, went the story, like as not, a member of that illustrious company would probably spring up with her. Although legend states that she was given membership for her many generous gifts to the community, more realistic thought suggests that the honor was bestowed to guarantee more favorable rates for the members of the department.

Just the same, her honorary appointment to the most prestigious fire department in the state brought respectability to Bulette. In the short history of Virginia City, no other female had been so publicly exalted. She took full advantage of it. Most other ladies of the trade scarcely ventured near the business district; Julia Bulette frequented the shops and stores as if she had married the mayor. She purchased a beautiful jet black phaeton, and to set it off, she added a team of perfectly matched white horses. This vehicle, with Bulette elegantly situated inside, appeared in all the parades and other fashionable get-togethers. In her splendid uniform, she appeared at all of the fires. She was seen at all of the proper charity functions, often donating money on behalf of herself and those in her employ. Then she was murdered.

On the morning of January 20, 1867, her body was discovered in the bed of her white cottage. Her furs and jewels, a collection rumored to be of epic proportions, had disappeared. Her murder created a furor. Engine Company Number One went into mourning. Julia Bulette was given the largest funeral in the history of Virginia City, a town known for its parades and celebrations. A brass band, two dozen draped carriages, and the men of Engine Company Number One, in full regalia, led the black, silver-handled coffin on its way to the cemetery; speeches lasting several hours were made over her grave. Almost every male in town expressed his sadness.

The good women of the Comstock, on the other hand, expressed anger, for the first time venting their frustrations publicly over "that Bulette woman." For years they had bristled when Bulette rode in her open carriage along the city's main street; they were appalled when she appeared at Piper's Opera House draped in jewels and furs. They had sought to discredit Bulette prior to her death but had gotten nowhere. Her popularity had kept their vehemence in check.

A transient, John Millaenin, was suspected of the murder. He was of the same nationality as Bulette and a dashing figure in his own right. Although he steadfastly maintained his innocence, protesting that he had loved her, within a few weeks he was brought to trial. The housewives of Virginia City mobilized.

They brought flowers to his cell -- at a time when flowers were a true rarity in the city. They brought a multitude of baked goods and homemade candy; they brought him wine. One woman even went so far as to bring him poetry. A reporter described the writing thus: "The meter was not very good, but the poem did say that by his efforts in ridding the town of 'that Bulette viper' -- the poetess rhymed 'viper' with 'righter' -- he had cleansed the name of Virginia City, and that he should be rewarded by the town's magistrates and not hanged by them."

But John Millaenin was sentenced to be hanged.

There was more than one reason for the sudden burst of feminine concern. John Millaenin was every bit as handsome as Bulette had been beautiful. He was dark, gracious, even debonair, urging the women not to cry. But they did.

On April 24, 1867, they lined the streets as the carriage with Millaenin, seated between two priests, made its way through the streets to the scaffold. Whereas the uniformed members of Virginia

City's engine company had provided the splendor for the burial procession of Julia Bulette, the National Guard and the National Militia provided the color for her murderer's procession to the scaffold. The balconies and streets were crowded with people from all over the Comstock; mines shut down so workers could attend the hanging; even the Chinese and Paiutes were in attendance. Picture postcards of Millaenin enjoyed brisk sales. Wagers were made on how long it would take for the killer to die.

The demeanor of John Millaenin was described by author Max Miller. "He carried his part splendidly," wrote Miller; "He did not falter on the steps. He conducted himself exactly as a woman's benefactor should do, even to his farewell address to the uplifted faces. His talk was one of praise for the virtue of the housewives of Virginia City, and of thanks for all they had done for him. He hoped that they would remember him always."

They did not, of course. The life and death of Julia Bulette far overshadowed that of her murderer. Today, no one knows the resting place of John Millaenin. As was his wish, he was buried in the Catholic cemetery, but the years and the elements have combined to obliterate its location.

Millaenin has faded into history, but not his victim. In fact, a famous mine was named after her, the remains of which can still be seen today. And it is that particular mine that provides one last bit of irony to the story of Julia Bulette. In later years it proved to be the hottest in the region, with temperatures reaching more than 120 degrees below ground. It is, perhaps, an appropriate epitaph for the most famous madam Nevada has ever seen.

Drivin' the Woolies

Strange places are cradles of fortune.
Back East, they might think it absurd
      That a man might find wealth --
      Yes, and wisdom, and health,
In a wagon that follows the herd.

A miner stalks off thru the desert,
In valleys and canyons to roam
      With a pick and a spade.
      When his fortune is made
He still thinks of a tent as a home.

This, too, is a cradle of fortune;
A canvas-roofed box upon wheels.
      There's no swivel chair here,
      And no desktop veneer,
When Dame Nature puts over her deals.

A lone herder's camp on the prairies
A place to be lonesome, and sleep
      And stand guard with a gun
      While the rain and the sun
Slowly build up a fortune in sheep.

Tho wealth brings him mansions and gardens,
Still dear to the heart of a man
      Is the canvas-topped crate
      On a windswept estate --
The old cradle where fortune began.

By the time "Cradle O' Fortune", by Gene Lindberg, appeared in the *Denver Post* in 1930, the era of the sheepman had long passed. The docile, submissive creatures had first come to America by way of Labrador as early as 1000 A.D., but they swiftly disappeared, prey to the wilds and the weather. In 1493, Columbus, on his second voyage to the New World, brought others which survived. The Spanish explorer, Francisco Coronado, brought a large band with him on his quest for the fabled Seven Cities of Cibola in the Southwest in 1540. Still, by 1800, there were no sheep in what would someday become known as Nevada.

But all that would soon change...

As much as it galls those who prefer legend to fact, gold to copper, and cattle to sheep, huge herds of the wooly creatures provided the first stable economy the region had yet known. As thousands of miners began scouring the desert for that elusive outcropping of quartz, there were scores of farsighted men who could see what others could not, that hungry miners had to eat, and the best way to get meat to the miners was to bring the market to them -- on the hoof.

But sheep are notoriously ignorant animals. Getting a herd of any size to Nevada was no easy task, and the trials of the early sheepmen rivaled even the tribulations of the Comstock miner.

For a sheep drive to be even moderately successful, sheepmen would amass a herd of no less than 12,000 animals. These, in turn, were divided into separate bands so that no group of sheep would travel over the same ground when en route to the diggings, for to do so would mean starvation to the stragglers in the rear.

Sheep rise early, with the dawn. By ten o'clock, however, especially in warm weather, sheep will "shade up," simply stop, and no amount of urging will move them forward. They remain in place until late in the afternoon when the weather cools. Old-timers are fond of saying that the Spanish got their habit of taking siestas from their sheep.

Tenderfeet have likened a sheep drive to that of cattle, but, in truth, there is little in common. After a late afternoon drive, sheep are bedded down for the night, often near water. But unlike cattle, sheep are often restless, rising and visiting the water hole endlessly. When this happens, seasoned herders usually forsake their own sleep and hit the trail for their destination, even in the dead of night.

Water is also a problem. Although sheep are second cousins to the camel -- they can go several days without water and often do so with no ill effects -- the only time sheep like to approach the wet stuff is to drink it. Sheep hate to cross even the shallowest waterway.

One herder recalled, "I'll never forget the Truckee River -- not much of a stream; it was low water and the sheep could just walk across it. But, oh no, they didn't want to get their feet wet! Them damned sheep! We had about three thousand of them to push across. They balked, and we held them right on the bank at the water's edge. We held 'em there all day and all night and all the next day until 'bout sundown. We thought we could starve 'em across. No deal. So we tied a bunch together, neck and neck, with lariat ropes, and drug 'em across the river. All the rest of the herd followed. Damndest thing I ever seen."

Chimed in another sheepherder, "Hell, that ain't nothin'! Worst I ever saw was the time we had only a small bunch, only about 500 head. We come to a little stream -- I'll swear it wasn't over forty feet across and real shallow, only about six or eight inches deep. Do you think we could get those dirty little woolies to cross it? No sir, not by a damn sight. So we drug some of them across by the hind leg and tied 'em to the brush on the other side. After that, we got about three or four hundred of them across -- almost the whole bunch, and they didn't even get wet above the knees. But then all of a sudden, they all ran back! Except the ones we'd left tied to the brush. We never did get 'em across. We cut the tied ones loose and let 'em come back. We had to drive the whole bunch upstream about four miles until we came to a bridge. Sheep sure are hell when it comes to water!"

Sheep wranglers learned early that the best way to move their sheep and supplies across the vast expanses of desert was with a pack mule, the mule being much heartier than the horse. And the early sheepmen also learned quickly that the Basques, those rugged individuals from the Pyrenees of western Europe, made the best caretakers, for they could endure the tremendous hardship and the maddening loneliness which were the constant companions of the sheepherders.

Sheep provided sustenance for the miners of both California and Nevada. During the five years between 1855 and 1860, not less than half a million sheep were driven west across the wilds of Nevada. They are all gone now, of course, those vast white herds of thousands grazing slowly across the landscape. And despite all the stories about cowboys, I suspect that true Nevadans sorely miss them.

The Best In the West

It was a showplace in the truest sense of the word. In its day, it played host to spectacular Shakespeare, bawdy melodrama, and fiery Wagnerian opera. Across its hallowed boards strode a Who's Who of world famous performers, people like Adah Isaacs Menkin, Henry Ward Beecher, Thomas Keene, and even the legendary Buffalo Bill. Nevada had never seen anything like it.

Today the casual visitor to Virginia City can still step inside historic Piper's Opera House. (Actually, it's the third theater to be built on the site, for fire destroyed the first two.) Resting on a hillside facing east, in worn but stately fashion, it looks imperiously out over what was once the richest piece of real estate on earth. On occasion, its walls still echo with the sounds of a small chamber orchestra or a violin recital, but nothing could match the Piper's of old.

For the most part, the majority of the early towns in the old west were starved for good entertainment. But not Virginia City. Almost overnight the city was swimming in gold and silver ore, and when the miners wanted something, they usually got it -- the expense be damned. And performers soon realized that playing Piper's Opera House could bring them more money than they had imagined.

It was the custom of the day to salute a performer, not with the mere clapping of hands, but by pounding one's fists or feet on the furniture or the floor. If the quality of a performance was better than average, the miners would shower the entertainer with fifty-cent pieces, the most popular coin of the day. The results were often staggering. Writer Dan DeQuille stated simply that "coins totalling almost $5,000.00 was not uncommon." And that kind of bonus was far from the ultimate; the true test of a performer's excellence was gauged in solid silver. According to DeQuille, a "bar weighing 50 ounces, highly polished and suitably engraved," was given at the end of a popular run. It is estimated that more than forty performers received the honor during the heyday of the Comstock.

In addition to the bonuses, the backstage treatment was often just as extraordinary, even for Virginia City. Wells Drury, a renowned editor of the period, told of the time when the famous actor Edwin Booth, the brother of Lincoln's assassin and the most popular actor of the time, appeared in a version of *Hamlet*. "When Booth requested a makeshift grave," said Drury, "he was astounded to learn that some of the men had built him a real one!" It seems that during the night workmen had actually cut a hole in the floor of the stage and burrowed down into very solid bedrock! Noted Drury, "It was the most formidable grave in the history of the theater."

Even William Frederick Cody, the famous Indian scout known as Buffalo Bill, played Piper's. Cody had been touring with a show called "The Red Right Hand" or "The First Scalp for Custer." Buffalo Bill's Wild West Show was a visual extravaganza with hundreds of performers and extras, real horses, and wagons; it usually required a large arena. There the performers would engage in mock battles featuring scores of cowboys and Indians, soldiers and settlers who would blaze away at each other with wild abandon. But the boys of the Comstock wouldn't hear of it. They wanted the Wild West Show on the stage at Piper's, not outdoors. At Piper's it was held. The staging, of course, left a lot to be desired. During one performance featuring a real-life frontier scout named Captain Jack Crawford, who had been assigned to General Crook in the United Sates Army's sortie against the Sioux, Captain Jack was so confused by all the action in such an enclosed space that he somehow managed to shoot himself in the groin, a fact that was related with much glee in the papers the following day.

Gone now is the fearful clash of Shakespearean swords. Gone are the rousing strains of Gilbert and Sullivan, the melodic offerings of a famous soprano. Gone are the raucous laughs and stomping feet, the boos and hisses of the melodrama. But Piper's Opera House still stands, a monument to a time and place that will never be seen again.

May They Rest in Peace

A colorful record of Nevada's past, not found in most history books, is recorded in two frequently overlooked sources of information: old newspaper obituaries and graveyard markers. The latter are often terse but revealing; the former are commonly peppered with editorial comment. Both often disclose the truth of whether the wild, wild west was indeed wild.

Visitors to the Silver State are fascinated by Nevada's graveyards, and rightly so. When one gazes downward at the time-trodden mounds of earth in those deserted, wind-swept gravesites, the weathered, crumbling monuments tell a tale of a bygone era.

Boot Hill, in the rough-and-tumble town of Pioche, provides insight into the violence that was early Nevada. Old-timers are fond of saying that more than 100 men were buried there before the first occupant was given the opportunity to die of "natural" causes. The markers visible today bear this out. Apparently it was particularly unhealthy to shoot one's mouth off to the officers of Pioche: "James Butler - 1871. Killed by officer Shea. Insulting and threatening language was the cause." Four years later, John Bass was buried: "He opened fire on some peace officers. Now here he lay."

Another grave marker simply reads: "Thomas Goldman - 1871. Killed by Morgan Courtney." Just a few paces away there is ample evidence that Courtney eventually received his comeuppance: "Morgan Courtney - 1873. Feared by some; detested by others. Shot 4 times in the back." It seems that some person or persons finally got a little tired of the murderous Courtney and decided to take matters into their own hands.

A walk through the graveyard of Pioche is a walk through a violent past. Many gravestones tell no more about a man buried there than by whom he was killed: "Thomas Gorson, Killed by Mike Casey." The tombstone over George Harris reveals a little more: "George

Harris - 1871. Killed by D.A. Myehdortt. Harris hit Myehdortt in the face." One poignant marker sheds light on the fact that Boot Hill was not exclusively reserved for men. It reads, "Fanny Patterson - July 12, 1872. They loved each other 'til death did them part. He killed her."

Many Boot Hill gravesites plainly bear the message of the lawlessness of the times. The marker for one James Whitlock, who was shot in 1870, reads, "Killed by James Maxwell. He made sure Whitlock would not testify in court." He surely did. And this: "Ur Warnock. Many arrests but no convictions." Sounds like someone got plenty tired of Ur getting off the hook and decided a little taste of vigilante justice was in order.

As the town of Pioche was fading, the boomtown of Tonopah was coming into its own. Here too is evidence of the harshness of the times. After a tremendous outbreak of fever in 1906, many graves such as this one appeared: "Naomio McGonagill. Died of the typhoid. Age 16." Fire broke out in Tonopah's Belmont mine five years later, and many gravestones mark the resting place of those who perished. Some, like William Murphy, were interned as genuine heroes: "Died February 23, 1911. Big Bill. Died in the Belmont Mine fire while helping others to escape." Dead men tell no tales, the saying goes, but their gravestones are not mute.

The other great source of information is the obituary columns of the day. In the late 1880's, these frequently included commentary about the character of the deceased and revealing bits of information about the circumstances of their demise, often ironic: "A.W. Abbott. He was a peacemaker in a fight in Ashley's Saloon." The *Lincoln County Record*, one of the state's oldest newspapers, reported that "Louis Bascon was killed at the home of H.A. Mason where he had asked young Ursula Mason to marry him. When she said 'no,' Bascon shot himself on the spot." The paper added wryly that the young girl in question was "only 16." The *Record* really indulged itself on the death of Mrs. Lewis Berndt: "She had violent, ungovernable passions and an unbridled tongue. She murdered her husband and then herself. Jealously was the motive."

Again, as with early tombstones, the obituaries underscored the violence of the times, but they also seemed to beg for further explanation: "J. Brown killed in Silver City, 1874. He was an innocent bystander killed in a mining dispute." What mining dispute? Who was involved? Who was at fault? And this one: "A Mr. Carol was killed near Ward. He was shot 18 times while trying to stop a stage coach robbery." Eighteen times? It sounds like he was the victim of a major massacre!

Was the wild, wild west really wild? Judge for yourself: John

Donohoe, a lawman, was "killed while escorting a prisoner to Hamilton. He was gunned down by 16 armed men." Here's another: "David Allen. Killed 1876 at Cajon in a shootout among sheepherders." Smoke Valley had an interesting one, two obituaries for the price of one. Seems that a fellow by the name of Chris Elkstein got into an argument with a man named Morton. According to the paper, "Morton was accused of taking too much notice of Chris' wife. Morton had a gun, Chris a Bowie knife. They found both men in a death lock." Finally, the demise of Thomas Dougherty in 1874, comes from Battle Mountain: "The same day he arrived in town from Salt Lake City, he planned to kill several people. He started with a Mister Kelly, but Kelly shot him first."

Some say that the wild American West was more fiction than fact, that violent gunfights and badmen were more figments of the imaginative talents of those who wrote dime novels and magazine articles than anything else. Still, Nevada's colorful history tells quite a different story, and it is mirrored in her obituaries, indelibly cast in the stones of her graveyards.

How to Make Water Run Uphill

The year was 1872. Three small, bustling cities were clinging precariously to the slopes of Mount Davidson. Virginia City and her sisters, Silver City and Gold Hill, separated by only a few hundred yards, were teeming with wealth. New ore deposits seemed to be unearthed almost daily.

The roads up the mountain were jammed with stagecoaches, wagon teams, men on foot, and men on horseback. The rush to Washoe was on! So overwhelming was the flood of humanity that Mark Twain wrote that it took him half an hour just to be able to cross Virginia City's main thoroughfare. More than thirty stagelines were now serving the city, and freight wagons snaked for miles all the way down the mountain to the valley floor.

But Mother Nature is a perplexing soul. On the one hand, she had provided a mountain of solid silver, the richest deposit of ore in the nation's history, some said. Despite her generosity, she failed to provide something just as precious, a continuous water supply. The three towns atop the mountain were drying up. Almost daily, the water supply was diminishing at a drastic rate. Mine owners and shop keepers, bankers and teamsters, instead of dancing with euphoria, were suddenly experiencing real panic.

In the initial days of the first gold and silver discoveries, a system of small reservoirs had been developed to catch the runoff from winter snowfalls. Dams were constructed across dry ravines, and tunnels were built to supply the towns. But this water supply was not only inadequate, it was proving to be downright dangerous. It was laced with arsenic and other minerals, and many early citizens slowly, painfully, died of the poisoning. Something had to be done. Immediately. Problem was, the closest supply of water was more than twenty-five miles away across the valley, high in the Sierra Nevada.

In 1872, the mine owners pooled their resources in a last-ditch attempt to solve their problem. They hired a renowned engineer, Herman Schussler of San Francisco. It was rumored that Schussler had done the impossible before. Perhaps....

The "impossible" facing the young engineer was staggering in its proportions. The water in the Sierra was not only miles away, it was separated by Washoe Valley, 2,000 feet below. The problem was not how to get the water down into the valley but how to get it to Virginia City, up another mountain more than 1500 feet high. Although there was no precedent for such an amazing feat of engineering, Schussler declared that he was up to the task. He designed a complicated, one-of-a-kind syphon, more than nine miles long. Then he set about making his dream come true.

Iron was imported from Ireland, then specially fashioned into pipe in San Francisco. It was no mean feat. The route of the syphon required it to pass over, around, and through such rugged terrain that each section of pipe had to be individually constructed to precise specifications so that, when lowered in place, it would fit perfectly. In addition, to utilize the principles of the basic syphon, the dimensions of each section had to be varied. At the top of the Sierra, the pipe was twelve inches in diameter and almost half an inch thick. As the water rushed down to the valley floor then up to the mountaintop at much lower pressure, the size of the pipe's walls had to be decreased dramatically. Its thickness now dropped to a mere sixteenth of an inch.

Somehow the "impossible" came to pass. Although the syphon was required to withstand pressures of up to 900 pounds per square inch, needed 1,475 sleeves, and required more than one million individual rivets, it was done. There had never been an engineering feat like it. There has never been one since.

But Schussler's problems were not over yet; he still needed an initial water supply on the Sierra side.

So a dam was created across a meadow on the eastern slope of the Tahoe Basin. The reservoir, named Marlette Lake after S.H. Marlette, Nevada's Surveyor General, soon rose majestically on the crown of the high Sierra. When filled to capacity, the storage basin would be almost fifty feet deep, would cover more than thirty acres, and it would hold more than two billion gallons of water. It was fed by an intricate network of flumes more than thirty-seven miles long. Several smaller reservoirs were created as a precautionary measure.

On the Virginia City side of the syphon there was still additional work to be done. Storage tanks had to be built at the eastern end of the pipeline and then water mains constructed to supply the cities. The work was frantic, around-the-clock, but it was done.

More than seventeen miles of water mains were built.

On August 1, 1873, Schussler's dream finally came true. With men stationed along the line with signal fires to alert him to trouble, water roared into the western end of the syphon. As air was forced ahead of the oncoming torrent of water, bystanders followed its raging path just by listening for the sound.

But would the rivets hold? Would the sleeves withstand the pressure? Had the iron been tempered enough to withstand the incredible pressure? Only Schussler seemed confident.

Suddenly, water came pouring into the storage tanks of Virginia City, and the town erupted in a tremendous celebration. Cannons were fired from the mountaintop; flags were hoisted in celebration; church and fire bells pealed out the news. Water! Precious, life-giving water had finally arrived on the Comstock Lode.

Schussler's dream resulted in the creation of the Virginia City Water Company. Incredibly, against all odds, he had managed to do what they said couldn't be done. His expenses for such a monumental and revolutionary undertaking were incredible as well. The entire project cost the mine owners a scant $3,000,000, a paltry sum when billions in ore was waiting deep underground.

Schussler had done it. The young, wild-eyed engineer had managed to make water, Nevada's most precious resource, actually run uphill...

The Legend of Fish Lake

A very small body of water, Fish Lake is located in the Columbus mining district, one of the richest in Nevada. In its time, it yielded more than seventy million dollars in gold and silver ore, making it second in riches only to fabulous Virginia City of Comstock fame.

The first prospectors to hit the area in 1864 were Mexican, and they found the going far from easy. Water had to be brought in by wagon, a distance of more than eight miles. It cost five cents a gallon. And if the flies, the ants, and the tarantulas didn't run the men off, the Indians did. In fact, after one particularly hair-raising confrontation, the miners completely abandoned the region and temporarily set up camp more than 100 miles away. From this relatively safe distance, they incorporated the district; when things quieted down, they returned to file their claims. Soon three raucous towns had sprung up, Candelaria, Belleville, and Columbus. The rush was on.

The name Fish Lake wasn't very fancy, but the lake became, in the words of a prominent judge, "a fashionable watering place for the District's elite." Though it was merely a tiny sheet of water in the relatively barren landscape, it was fed by warm springs which even in summer offered a welcome respite from the searing heat.

But the legends of the Paiute Indians preserve the fact that, long before the coming of the white men, Fish Lake was a favorite resort of their ancestors. The shores were dotted with their picturesque wickiups, and in the evening the water came alive with the children of the valley, enthusiastically engaged in water sports. And then it happened.

It was back in 1873, when a brave by the name of Nak-Tah-Kotch came to the lake with several of his wives and a couple of small children. One was an infant carried in a wicker basket. As the heat

105

of the day bore down, one of the women placed the basket in a comfortable position propped up against a sagebrush near the water's edge. She then busied herself in preparing a frugal meal of dried venison, pine nuts, and out-chu, a potato-like plant that grew wild in the area.

Suddenly she was startled by a child's cry; she turned and watched in horror as the basket tumbled into the water. As the infant screamed, a gust of wind moved the basket swiftly out onto the lake. She sprang to the rescue, diving into the water without hesitation. But in her frenzy she immediately sank to the bottom. Nak-Tah-Kotch plunged in to assist her; in desperation the woman flung her arms around his neck, and, clasping him in a death grip, pulled them both to their deaths. The lightweight basket floated out into the middle of the lake with its tiny cargo.

By this time the rest of the tribe had congregated along the banks. The Indians were frightened. They believed that the Great Spirit held them somehow in disfavor. They refused to try to rescue the infant as slowly the blackness of night fell over Fish Lake. The superstitious Paiutes could only watch and wait.

When the moon rose, the wicker basket was discovered nestled safely in the rushes once again at water's edge. The baby was fast asleep, blissfully unaware of the danger or the tragedy that had occurred. She was taken from the basket, and in a solemn ceremony, she was adopted by new parents. From that day forward she was known as Tah-Peta, meaning Saved-By-The-Moon, and she became a favorite of the tribe.

Nevertheless, the die had been cast. The Indians believed that the Great Spirit had given them a sign, a sign of displeasure. Fearing the wrath of their Almighty, they left Fish Lake, never to return. It was the last time the Indians were ever sighted in the area.

But the whites feared neither the power of the Great Spirit nor the wrath of the Indians. Even the possibility of an Indian uprising was not enough to stay the onslaught of men whose visions were clouded with the promise of wealth.

Today the miners and prospectors are gone. The fabulous wealth has long since disappeared. Little remains of the frenzy that accompanied the miners who swarmed over the area or of the peaceful Indian tribe that once camped beside the waters. But the story of the tragedy lives on, in the folklore of Nevada's Paiutes. Today, they still speak softly to their children of the time when the Great Spirit was displeased, of the time when He swallowed up two of their people and banished the remainder of the tribe from Fish Lake forever.

The Jewel of the Sierra

Mark Twain called it "a jewel in the crown of the Sierra." Nestled comfortably near the dome of one of the most formidable mountain ranges in the west, Lake Tahoe glimmers majestically, attracting thousands of tourists annually. It is to the city of Reno what Lake Mead is to Las Vegas, a glittering diamond set in a mostly-desert state.

Tahoe has always been a playground, particularly so in the early days of the Silver State when those wishing to escape the harshness of life in the mines would flock to its high-mountain shores for a much-needed respite. One writer recounts the scene in the late 1800's: "...we hasten on board the *Governor Stanford*, and Tahoe, the great mountain sea, glistens like burnished glass. Waveless, unbroken, as far as the eye can see, it presents the same polished surface. The steamer's prow cleaves the deep, blue waters so quietly and smoothly that we can fancy ourselves floating in air. The pretty lake steamer skims along at the rate of more than 12 miles an hour and we shall cover the 100-mile trip in 8 hours."

That 100 mile outing was a popular pastime for many visitors, including Mark Twain, who often escaped the hectic pace of Virginia City to "hide out" in the Grand Central Hotel. The establishment boasted the finest in accommodations, including a bowling alley, luxurious baths, croquet fields, even its own telegraph line. Heady stuff, considering the times.

Tahoe is a lake which spawns legends. For a time it was rumored that a giant sea serpent lived in the depths. Even today, "Tahoe Tessie" t-shirts can be purchased in lakeside gift shops. There were good reasons for the rumors. Until recently, the lake's bottom, which drops to more than 1400 feet, had never been charted; the temperatures, always cold and never varying winter or summer, made exploration almost impossible.

Another popular myth held that Tahoe was connected by a deep underground shaft to the mines of Virginia City. Newspapers espoused the theory when the body of a well-known Tahoe resident was found in one of Virginia City's deep mine shafts. The body had been spirited there by an underground river, wrote the paper.

Then there was the case of Captain Dick. Dick had been the captain of a man-of-war during the War of 1812; in retirement he had forsaken the open sea for the land-locked lake high in the Sierra. He was an eccentric, given to extensive bouts with demon whiskey.

But folks thought him really strange when he settled in at Emerald Bay and began to build his own grave. On a rocky island, he chiseled out a hole, then built a stone house over it. He even erected an elaborate cross.

Perhaps Dick knew that the end was coming; shortly after the completion of his stone house, he disappeared. His boat was found, but not his body. One old-timer is convinced that today Dick rests, not in his carefully prepared crypt, but in 1200 feet of water: "Captain Dick's body is still there, necessarily in a perfect state of preservation on account of the intense cold. It will never rise to the surface."

But there is another side to Tahoe of which most people today are unaware. At one time, the famous lake was even more famous as a breadbasket for much of northern Nevada and California. Fourteen tons of Nevada butter were produced there during the 1870's, and they cost an incredible ten cents a pound. Some claimed it was the richest butter ever produced in the west. Hay was another principle product. Eight hundred tons were harvested annually in the lake valley, and those brought more than thirty dollars a ton, an exorbitant sum at the time. Fishing was profitable as well. At a time when Nevada's top miners were making no more than five dollars a day, fishermen on the lake were pulling in an average of sixty pounds of trout daily, which were sold for as much as fifteen cents a pound.

It was lumbering that really put Lake Tahoe on the map, a fact that many of today's environmentalists would just as soon forget. During the heyday of the silver mines in Virginia City and Gold Hill, the shores of the lake and much of the surrounding countryside were raped and pillaged in the frantic search for lumber. Even today, the signs of the rampant lumbering are still evident. As you drive up to the lake from the Nevada side, it looks as though someone placed a giant bowl over the crest of the mountain and then proceeded to carelessly shear away the ancient growth.

Someone did. In 1875 alone, more than twenty-nine million board feet of lumber were harvested from Lake Tahoe's shores. So desperate were the miners for timber to shore tunnels, for construction, and for firewood, that giant flumes were constructed to whisk the logs down the mountainside from the lake to the valley floor. In fact, flying logs sometimes made the journey from California to Nevada downright perilous! The giant flumes or chutes often towered as much as 200 feet in the air and occasionally spanned the wagon route across the mountains. Two businessmen on their way to Virginia City recalled a harrowing experience that almost cost them their lives.

As their carriage rounded a bend on the eastern slopes, they suddenly heard a deafening roar. Looking up, they saw a gigantic log plummeting down the chute. Their peril was immediately evident. The careening log was about to leave the chute, jump the road, and crash into the Truckee River. The men leaped from their carriage -- not a moment too soon. The log roared from the chute at breakneck speed, taking the carriage with it. The horses were crushed instantly.

Lake Tahoe. A spectacular mountain lake with an even more spectacular history. It fed the miners during the state's infancy and provided the mines with the lumber necessary to harvest its vast store of underground wealth. Today, the lake is still, as Mark Twain described, a jewel, especially for the desert state of Nevada.

Sutro's Folly

Born in Prussia, in 1830, Adolph Sutro studied mining and engineering in Europe. Armed with his education and more than a few dreams, he arrived in San Francisco in 1851. Eight years later, hearing of the fabulous silver strike in Virginia City, he packed up his wife and six children and set out to make a name for himself. Arriving on the Comstock, he built a quartz mill on the banks of the Carson River. It was an auspicious move for both Sutro and Nevada.

Those were fabulous times. The deep underground mines of Virginia City were yielding more gold and silver than any other operation on earth. The shafts were dug 500, 600, 700, and finally to the incredible depth of more than 1,000 feet. That's when the trouble began.

At 1,000 feet, the temperature in the mines rose to more than 120 degrees. Miners worked half-naked, chewing on ice in a desperate but futile effort to keep cool. In some shafts, they could work no more than half an hour before the intense heat drove them, exhausted, to the surface. To make matters worse, mysterious underground streams would flood the shafts, making it necessary to employ giant pumps that operated continuously day and night. Occasionally a miner's pick would break through a wall, and a torrent of scalding water would come streaming through, drowning the hapless men in the process. To many, it seemed that the mining operations on the Comstock would have to come to a halt.

Enter Adolph Sutro, a man with a vision. Sutro believed that a huge tunnel could be built from the banks of the Carson River up and into the mine shafts under Mount Davidson. The tunnel would serve several purposes. It would drain the water that was hindering the deepest mining operations and provide much-needed ventilation for the foul, stagnant air that collected in the shafts. Just as importantly, it would provide a means to move both men and materials to the

111

surface quickly and efficiently, without having a long haul straight up to the surface.

It was a good idea, of course, but most thought that it simply couldn't be done. "Pure speculation," they said. But the idea did attract the attention of William Ralston, the head of San Francisco's powerful Bank of California, and the manager of his Virginia City branch, William Sharon, who would go on to serve Nevada as a United States Senator. With letters of support, Sutro approached the Nevada Legislature and was given a franchise to begin his operations.

But the amount of money required was mind-boggling, particularly for the times. Sutro estimated that construction would cost in excess of $3,000,000. Armed with more letters, he went east where he was able to obtain the blessing of the United States Congress and more than a smattering of financial interest from such rich investors as Cornelius Vanderbilt and J.P. Morgan. But just as he was about to receive the necessary loans, Ralston and Sharon were having second thoughts. The Bank of California, under the astute guidance of Ralston and Sharon, had for some time a virtual monopoly on mine production on the Comstock. Based on the contract provisions that had been granted to Sutro, they knew that Sutro's tunnel would make him a fabulously rich man. Surely, they reasoned, he would become a powerful threat to the Bank of California's financial supremacy. The two withdrew their backing, even going so far as to send telegrams now calling Sutro's plan, Sutro's "folly." Refused financial aid in America, Sutro went to Europe in search of support. But when a war on the continent threatened, he returned to the United States empty-handed. Men would have to die before his work could begin.

On April 4, 1869, the shrill cry of warning whistles broke the crisp, clear morning air. The Yellow Jacket Mine was on fire! As giant clouds of smoke burst out of the shaft, burning cinders and chunks of wood exploded from the connected openings of the Kentuck and Crown Point mines. The fumes and flames were erupting from 900 feet below. More than forty men were burned alive.

But in the horror of tragedy, Sutro saw his chance. He printed handbills inviting all underground workers to attend a meeting at Maguire's Opera House. He told the stunned workmen that a tunnel was the only true hope of preventing future disaster. At meeting's end, he had a pledge of $50,000 in gold. Adolph Sutro set out to make his dream come true.

Work began on October 19, 1869, near the present town of Dayton. More than nine years later it was complete. Whistles blew and cannons were fired as Sutro's men broke through into a shaft of the Savage mine more than 1600 feet below the surface. It was truly a monumental achievement -- a four mile tunnel driven through solid rock at a pace of sometimes less than 150 feet a month! But the Prussian engineer had done it.

Within a few years, he would sell his share in the Sutro Tunnel project and retire to San Francisco. He invested shrewdly in real estate and served as that city's mayor from 1894 until his death in 1898. Adolph Sutro left his mark indelibly on the Comstock. His vision made it possible for the rich mining operations to continue for only a few more years, but productive years they were, yielding many more millions for the owners. But perhaps his biggest legacy is that he was a man who believed that you don't have to take "no" for an answer.

Another Humorist on the Comstock

Without a doubt, the most famous humorist in Nevada's history is Mark Twain. Although his tenure in the Silver State was actually quite short, Nevadans still hold him in awe. After all, didn't he get his start as a cub reporter on Virginia City's famous *Territorial Enterprise*? Doesn't that give Nevada some bragging rights?

But Twain's prominence and his knack for grabbing headlines only served to place other writers of the period in history's shadow. There were others far more accomplished at the time, like Twain's own contemporary on the *Enterprise*, Dan DeQuille. And there were others who were far better humorists.

A case in point: Fred Hart. "He had a boisterous braggadocio and the gift for elaborating a tale," wrote Jake Highton in *Nevada Newspaper Days*. Fred Hart, today a virtual unknown, became one of the most popular humorists in Nevada's history, Wrote Richard Lillard, "The only kind of literary man that the mineral frontier really understood or encouraged or tolerated was the humorist. Simply, he best articulated the local sense of fun."

"Fun" was the key word in many of the stories contained in early newspapers, and Fred Hart was the unchallenged king of sagebrush humor. He constantly poked fun at whatever he came across and saw no reason to pull any of his punches.

One of his most famous pieces took aim at the Nevada legislature, and that aim was deadly. Hart told the story of a doctor who treated a patient injured in a mine cave-in. The miner was suffering from a fractured skull, and the physician was forced to clean "three or four pounds of gravel" from the patient's brains. While the doctor was washing the brains, the man spied a few of his friends across the street and simply wandered out of the office, leaving his brains behind. After several months, the doctor came across his former patient on Main Street and asked why the man had not returned for his brains. "Don't want 'em," the man replied. "Why not?" the doctor asked. "Wal, you see, I'm running for office now and I don't really need 'em. Got no use for 'em. Fact is, they'd actually be an encumbrance, under the circumstances."

Hart began his illustrious career reporting for Austin's *Reese River Reveille* where his job ranged from "writing an advertisement about a lost dog," to "heavy dissertations on leading topics." But the town of Austin, once the center of much of Nevada's mining activity, had long since begun to fade. As the mines and miners moved on, the town became, according to one reporter, "more than a little dull."

But Hart had the uncanny ability to create news where none existed. His attention centered immediately on the Sazerac Lying Club, a group of the town's leading citizens who gathered in the Sazerac Saloon (named for a popular brandy) and swapped tall tales. Hart realized right away that he could turn "whoppers" into news items, and he began to do so without even a twinge of guilt. He would later write, "I am personally acquainted with some of the most prominent citizens of the Pacific Coast, who have made colossal fortunes simply by lying...by doctoring the truth about stock and mines; and those men are respected and looked up to, courted and flattered, called smart, and good businessmen." Hart sharpened his pen and proceeded to do more of the same.

A typical Hart "news" item: "REJECTED -- The name of Eli Perkins was proposed for membership in the Sazerac Lying Club last night. The applicant was rejected on the grounds that the applicant's lies were utterly improbable ones and came under the rule that no member shall be allowed to tell a lie that might have been true had such a thing ever happened."

After a Fourth of July celebration in 1877, during which the members of the Liar's Club became so drunk that they needed two days to recuperate, Hart again poked fun in print. The Club would not meet, Hart reported, "until the president's eyes are able to appear in public without a fresh beef over them."

The group's legendary drinking bouts were a constant source of inspiration for Hart. He once reported that an Austin summer was so hot that he had discovered one of the club members actually drinking water! Tongue firmly planted in his cheek, Hart wrote, "This revolutionary act was performed in secret so as not to set a bad example for the other members." He added that an investigation was under way to learn the extent of the use of "forbidden water."

By 1880, Hart had moved on like many other Austin residents before him. That year found him in Virginia City, this time at the helm of the *Territorial Enterprise*, still the most famous newspaper in the state. Here his razored pen took on the political establishment.

One of his first sorties concerned the race for United States Senate. James Fair, one of the original Bonanza Kings, had entered the race and was considered a sure win. Undaunted, Hart countered with an editorial entitled "Slippery Jim", and proceeded to lambast the would-be Senator, reminding him, in twenty-one damning paragraphs, of many previous but not forgotten transgressions.

Hart should have stuck to humor. He had forgotten that the owners of the *Enterprise* were none other than mining baron John MacKay and...the illustrious Jim Fair. MacKay went storming into Hart's office demanding to know the identity of the "sun of a gun" who wrote "all this trash" about his partner. Hart managed to keep his job only by promising not to be so frank in the future.

But Hart was not quiet for long. He soon printed another editorial entitled "The Alta Steal" in which he detailed how the stockholders of that prominent company had been robbed of hundreds of thousands of dollars through fraudulent stock manipulations. This time MacKay almost had a coronary, for the corporation was a huge advertiser, its principals close friends. Wisely, Hart packed his bags and headed on to San Francisco, having learned the sober truth that freedom of the press was usually only "free" to the press's owner.

Fred Hart would die of Bright's Disease in Sacramento, California, in 1897. Until his death, his lively editorials continued to tell the "whole" truth about the inner workings of Pacific mining operations. His columns about the Sazerac Lying Club were turned into a popular book, so successful it survived three separate printings.

Although Fred Hart has long since been forgotten, overshadowed by the works of his famous contemporary, Mark Twain, his work lives on. Perhaps Comstock reporter Alf Doten said it best. Writing Hart's obituary, he recalled Hart's famous collection of "liar's" stories. Wrote Doten, "[They] are an enduring monument to the literary genius of Fred Hart."

Rollin' on the River

When people think about the early pioneers and the settling of the west, visions of covered wagons, stagecoaches, and railroads spring to mind. But even in early Nevada, regarded by most as just a vast desert, the swiftest and usually the safest means of travel was on the river. Today the mighty Colorado River is but a shadow of its former self. Harnessed by massive dams and drained by thirsty cities, the Colorado is in danger. But in 1872, that was hardly the case.

For a time, the river was the lifeline for the early settlements of southern Nevada. Coal from New Mexico was shipped north to fuel isolated mining operations. Even a locomotive was shipped up river for use in one of the mines. Salt, hay, and farm produce were shipped south from Nevada ranches. The Colorado was to Nevada what the Mississippi was to Louisiana.

But travel up and down the river left a lot to be desired. Rapids proved to be such a constant danger that special ringbolts were fashioned to canyon walls. Upon approaching a dangerous portion of the river, the crew would wrestle a heavy cable out in front of the boat and affix it to the side of the canyon. Then, with the help of a steam winch, the boat would pull itself up and over the raging waters.

Crews were particularly difficult to find in sparsely populated Nevada, and local Indians were often used. The Indians, however, too often proved unreliable. W.S. Mills, the Superintendent of the Southwestern Mining and Milling Company which had an extensive operation in El Dorado Canyon, one day reported that the Indian laborers had simply disappeared. Wrote Mills, "most of them have gone to Las Vegas to eats grapes, melons, etc."

The searing heat made passage on the river almost unbearable. One traveller, Martha Summerhayes, described her own excursion on the river in the 1870's: "We had staterooms, but could not remain in them long at a time, on account of the intense heat. There was no ice and consequently, no fresh provisions." She recalled that the heat was so intense that she was tempted to throw herself into the river at every turn: "The dining room was hot. The metal handles of the knives were uncomfortably warm to the touch; and even the wooden arms of the chairs felt as if they were slowly igniting...."

The crew battled the constantly shifting river bottom on a daily basis. "As the river narrowed, the trip was enlivened by the constant danger of getting aground on the sand bars which are so numerous in this mighty river....The deckhands...stood ready with long poles in the bow, to jump overboard when we struck a bar, and, by dint of pushing and reversing the engines, the boat would swing off."

But even in the best of times, travel by steamship was unreliable. Superintendent Mills wrote a scathing letter to one steamship company whose irregular schedule threatened to close his milling operation: "The last information from the steamer [was that] she was at Needles on the 16th and had on board 75 cords of wood for us and was loading our powder, barley, etc. We don't know what has become of her since."

Mills had expected the steamship carrying his precious supplies by January. He wrote, "In the fore part of February, [they] notified us that the steamer would leave Yuma for Eldorado Canyon about February 15th. On the 16th of February they wrote us that the steamer would leave Yuma for the Canyon on February 25th. On the first of March they wrote us that it would leave on March 2nd. [Finally] on the 16th of March, Captain Mellon wrote us that the steamer was there loaded for this company. This is our last information on the subject."

When four months had passed and there was still no sign of the steamship, Mills prepared to close down his mining operation: "Unless it appears soon we shall have to suspend for want of powder, fuel, etc. But we are anxiously looking down the river in hopes." The steamer eventually arrived, four and a half months late.

Despite the hardships of river travel and the unreliability of her steamships, commerce on the Colorado continued until just after the turn of the century. With the coming of the railroad in 1905, it became more practical to service the mining camps by land rather than ply the waters of the Colorado. The last of the boats to sail the river was aptly named *Searchlight*, after the southern Nevada town of the same name. The hardy ship had served the camp for several decades.

The Colorado River has changed drastically since the glory days of the early steamboats. Even the town of Callville, established by Mormon engineers in 1864 as a landing and warehousing center, now lies submerged under Lake Mead, which was created by the building of Hoover Dam. Gone now are the bolts that used to protrude from the canyon walls. Gone are the colorful plumes of steam that drifted up from the riverbanks. Gone are the haunting echoes of the steamwhistle. Still, for a while at least, travel by steamboat was the only way to go.

Sarah Winnemucca: Paiute Princess

Few of the western Indian tribes have set down their heritage in anything but oral legend, stories passed from one generation to another, a rich heritage too often lost. But Nevada in the 1880's had a chronicler who remembered vividly the early days before the coming of the white man: Sarah Winnemucca.

Born about 1844, near Humboldt Lake, she was the daughter of powerful Paiute Chief Winnemucca, and her Indian name was Thocmetony -- Shell Flower. As she grew, so did her association with the whites who were now dashing headlong across the deserts of her native Nevada in search of gold and silver. So adept was she at her mastery of the English language that she served as a guide and interpreter during the Bannock Wars in the summer of 1878. Her assistance led to a series of lectures; she traveled the country extensively telling the story of her people. Those who met her and heard her speak called her "Princess," and she seemed to dote on the title, wearing white clothing and eventually marrying a white Montana rancher, Lambert Hopkins.

While on an excursion to the east, she made the fortuitous acquaintance of two wealthy ladies of Boston, Elizabeth Peabody and Mary Mann, who took the Indian woman under their wing. They not only encouraged her to continue to tell the country about her life among the Paiutes, they suggested she write a book, offering to assist with editing and publishing. *Life Among the Paiutes: Their Wrongs and Claims* was the eventual result. It was published in 1883 and widely circulated, especially along the eastern seaboard. It has provided some of the most vivid recollections of early Nevada in existence.

Sarah told of the beginning of the world as the Indians knew it, a world consisting of merely six people, two adults and four offspring, two boys and two girls: "One girl and one boy were dark and the others were white." According to the legend told by her grandfather, Chief Truckee:

> They were cross to one another and fought, and our parents were very much grieved....the father and mother saw that they must separate their children; and then our father took the dark boy and girl, and the white boy and girl, and asked them, 'Why are you so cruel to each other?' They hung down their heads and would not speak....So he separated his children by a word. He said, 'Depart from each other, you cruel children; -- go across the mighty ocean and do not seek each other's lives.'
>
> So the light girl and boy disappeared by that one word, and their parents saw them no more, and they were grieved, although they knew their children were happy. And by-and-by the dark children grew into a large nation; and we believe it is the one which we belong to,...

Although no one in early Nevada had even seen a white man until the early 1830's, it was the sacred belief of Sarah's people that the whites would return one day, and they would be welcomed with open arms. Those of the dark skin and those of the white would be a family once more. Her account recalls that day when the first wagon train of settlers wound its way slowly down the Humboldt River through the camp of her grandfather, Chief Truckee: "When the news was brought to my grandfather, he asked what they looked like? When told they had hair on their faces, and were white, he jumped up and clasped his hands together, and cried aloud, -- 'My white brothers, -- my long-looked for white brothers have come at last!'" He went to meet them and approached them in friendly greeting but was made to keep his distance. Wrote Sarah, "He knew not what to do. He had expected so much pleasure in welcoming his white brothers to the best in the land, that after looking at them sorrowfully for a little while, he came away quite unhappy."

The old chief still refused to believe that these whites were not part of the original universe. He followed the train for days, camped nearby at night and made repeated entreaties of friendship. But it was not to be. Continued Sarah, "my grandfather left them, saying, 'Perhaps they will come again next year.'"

The whites would come again the following year, but this time in ever-increasing numbers and displaying ever-increasing hostility.

Word had raced east that a great gold discovery had been made along the banks of the American River in California. It seemed as though half the white nation was suddenly on the move. It would never be the same for the Winnemucca family. In an endless search for firewood, whites would cut down almost every tree in the Paiute land, including the pine nut. Animals from the trains pulled the scant prairie grass up by the roots until lush beds of clover that once sustained the tribes of the region were virtually non-existent. Although some of the first wagon trains through the territory were friendly and offered to trade for pots, pans, and trinkets of little value, the onslaught of western movement had begun.

Sarah's grandfather never gave up his vision of a reunited nation in the Utah Territory, but it was a dream that never came true. Whites continued to swarm through the region, destroying the Paiute land in their hasty search for riches. Sarah spent almost a decade fighting the government policies established toward her people but did not live to see the fruition of her efforts. It is a tale of tragedy -- when two cultures meet without realizing the ties of their ancient past.

A Difficult Man to Like

"I've always built my success on other men's failures," bragged Jim Fair, and it was true. Although he would go on to amass a fortune estimated to be almost fifty million dollars, his money brought him neither friendship nor respect. But Jim Fair couldn't have cared less. Stories of his greed and egocentric obsession with making money are legion. Fellow Comstock millionaire John MacKay recalled the time when Fair was asked to give one of his most loyal workers a pay raise. Replied Fair, "A hungry hound hunts best."

Even members of his immediate family were not immune. In later years, upon learning that the stock in the Gould and Curry mine was about to plummet and anxious to unload his own shares, Fair even swindled his own wife. He slyly inquired how much she had in her savings account; then he casually mentioned that stock in the Gould and Curry was about to "go through the roof." While his wife invested her entire life savings in Gould and Curry stock, which caused a temporary rise in values, Fair sold his own at a substantial profit. When the stock eventually dropped to nothing, he appeared unconcerned that his wife had lost her entire savings. He simply said, "My dear, I'm afraid you will never be a speculator."

Who was this ruthless man who amassed such an incredible fortune and was so universally despised?

Like his fellow millionaire, John MacKay, James Fair was born in Dublin. When he was a child, his family emigrated to New York, and after several years on a farm in Illinois, Fair set out to make his fortune in the gold fields of California. For almost ten years, he searched the streams and gullies of the region. He was one of the few who struck it rich although the means he used were hardly revolutionary. One day he spied two Indians who had come into camp to trade for supplies. Upon closer examination, he learned that the Indians had gold to trade. When the Indians departed, Fair and a companion followed them to their location and managed to make off with more than $180,000 in ore. The theft marked the beginning of his eventual fortune.

Unlike others who returned home when the promise of riches had been exhausted, James Fair continued on. Although the work was backbreaking, to Fair it was no more than a means to an end. And for James Fair, that meant that someday he would be as rich as Midas. With typical guile, he salted his Angel's Camp gold mine and sold it to an eastern tenderfoot. Already a wealthy man, he headed for still richer pastures, the Comstock Lode of Nevada.

By the time Jim Fair arrived in 1865, the Comstock was suffering from growing pains. Most of the silver that lay near the surface had already been extracted. Few suspected that the surface of Mount Davidson had barely been scratched.

But Fair had not spent an idle moment while he was prospecting in California. He had studied quartz mining and devoured any information he could find about the deep underground mines of Austria and Hungary. His new-found knowledge, coupled with his extensive gift of gab, soon landed him a job as superintendent of the Ophir mine.

The following year, Fair was hired by the trustees of the Hale and Norcross, a once profitable strike which had since fallen on hard times. Fair was convinced that the mine would prove to be rich beyond imagination. He asked his fellow Irishman, John MacKay, to have a look. MacKay concurred with Fair's assessment, and the two men, with the help of two San Francisco bartenders-turned-financiers, Flood and O'Brien, managed to take control of the apparently failing property. Two weeks later, the news hit: a new strike at the Hale and Norcross was proving to be the biggest in the history of the Comstock Lode. Overnight, Fair and MacKay, along with their San Francisco partners, were rich.

This success would soon be overshadowed by yet another bold move. The four men wisely invested almost all of their new-found wealth in another claim that traditionally had yielded little. Soon they were the proud owners of the Consolidated-Virginia, a shaft that appeared to many to be borrasca.

For months the men worked the Consolidated-Virginia. Soon backers and speculators began to worry, first silently then publicly. If silver wasn't found soon, the entire operation would collapse. It was then that MacKay and Fair discovered a solid wall of silver. The Consolidated-Virginia, of which the four men owned more than seventy-five percent, would prove to be the richest discovery in the history of North America.

Nevertheless, by 1877, the mines, extraordinarily rich though they were, were finally exhausted. Flood, O'Brien, and MacKay, seeing the handwriting on the wall, began to divest themselves of their mining interests. Fair turned toward the political arena. He wasn't well-liked, but he knew what the miners wanted, and he knew how to buy it. Although he was facing the formidable William Sharon for the Nevada Senate seat, Fair overwhelmed the banker by spending almost $350,000 on his campaign, some of it to openly buy votes.

Fair was undistinguished in the halls of Congress. By the second year, he hardly showed up at all, preferring instead to spend his time in his office, feet propped up on his desk, a brandy bottle nearby. He liked to regale other senators with tales of "his" discovery of the Comstock Lode.

While in Washington, Fair would incur the wrath of his most faithful partner, John MacKay. Fair had departed leaving his wife without a source of income. When Mrs. Fair appealed to MacKay for assistance, she got it, but MacKay seldom talked to his partner again.

Fair continued to "play" while in the nation's capital and soon the word reached Virginia City that he was "consorting with other women." In the subsequent divorce trial, several ladies testified as to Fair's adultery, and Mrs. Fair was awarded $4,750,000, the largest divorce settlement in the nation's history. Fair left Washington and Virginia City as well, never to return.

He knew better than to run again for the Senate. Instead, he returned to San Francisco where he began buying income properties. By 1879, he owned more than sixty acres of prime real estate in the very heart of the city. In typical Scrooge-like fashion, he demanded that upkeep on all his properties be handled by his renters.

Eventually, time, alcohol, and long working hours took their toll. On December 29, 1894, James Fair died. He was only sixty-three.

But what followed kept Fair in the limelight for another decade. Soon suits were brought contesting Fair's will, and an obscene number of women came forth to claim that they were a mistress, a long lost daughter, or a paramour who had been given the promise of marriage. More than two million dollars were spent in deciding the outcome, and so many lawyers were involved that a San Francisco paper reported that "a substantial part of the Fair fortune will be devoted to the philanthropy of a particularly heart-warming kind. It will enable nearly a score of rich but deserving attorneys to spend the balance of their lives on the lap of luxury."

James Fair. He was a skinflint, a womanizer, a boozer, and a cheat. But for almost half a century this strange millionaire remained front page news across the nation. And in Virginia City, Nevada, the place where it all began, he remains to this day the man known disparagingly as "Slippery Jim."

John MacKay: Man of Paradox

A stranger went to San Francisco's Palace Hotel looking for multi-millionaire mine owner John MacKay. When he inquired at the front desk, he was informed that the wealthy man was in the adjacent bar with several of his friends.

"But how will I know him?" asked the newcomer.

"Easy," replied the hotel man, "he'll be the one who says nothing and pays the bill."

John MacKay is a true Nevada legend. Born in Dublin in 1831, he emigrated to New York when still a child. Uneducated, even in his forties he was occasionally found reading elementary grammar books. He arrived in Virginia City, Nevada, penniless; when he left, he was making more than ten thousand dollars a day. Unlike many men who rise phoenix-like to glory, John MacKay remained a quiet man, spurning lavish dinner parties and public functions, preferring to retire each day to a single room in whatever city he was staying. Much has been written about him, yet he remains a curious enigma, a man who throughout his colorful career confounded even those who knew him well.

He held the belief that to loan money to a man "took away the man's pride," yet he loaned out more than five million dollars during his lifetime and once wrote off more than a million dollars in bad debts to personal friends.

He scorned doctors. Even after he became wealthy, he often made them wait forever for their money. On one occasion, after an old adversary shot him in the back on a San Francisco street, he sued the doctors who operated on him and succeeded in getting them to reduce their bill.

He installed new-fangled elevators in many of his buildings, yet stubbornly refused to use them himself, preferring to bound up and down stairs for exercise.

131

He was entirely without ego, and his generosity was enormous, provided he could be guaranteed anonymity. When it was discovered that he had been underwriting a local Nevada hospital for years, he threatened to stop his payments if the matter ever became public. When an old friend embezzled some money and left town leaving his wife behind, MacKay one day appeared on her doorstep. "I am convinced that your husband cannot possibly be guilty," he confided to the grieving woman. "I know he must have left that money here in this house." Sending the young wife to search her husband's clothes, he slipped an envelope into a coat that had been hanging in the vestibule. When the wife returned having found nothing, MacKay suggested searching the vestibule as well. There she found the envelope which contained enough to cover the embezzlement and additional living expenses.

He scorned most forms of relaxation and entertainment, yet became one of the founders of the world-famous Metropolitan Opera in New York.

He was fond of boxing and maintained a boxing ring in the basement of his San Francisco banking firm. He allowed James Corbett, who ultimately became the world champion "Gentlemen Jim," to train there. Yet, when he asked Corbett to choose between a career in boxing and a job as his clerk and Corbett chose boxing, MacKay refused to see him again for many years.

Although his wife hired a butler to do whatever butlers do, MacKay refused to utilize the man's services, forcing the hapless servant to simply follow him around at a hectic pace.

He could afford the most luxurious accommodations of the day, yet he preferred common hotel rooms and maintained them in almost every city he visited on a regular basis. When fire devastated his Virginia City mansion, he simply moved to a hotel rather than rebuild the home. He shared that same room with a miner down on his luck.

His wife traveled constantly and maintained an elegant residence in Paris, yet MacKay seldom visited. When he did manage an annual trip to Europe, he left instructions with his San Francisco business manager, Dick Dey, to wire him almost immediately with some convenient excuse for him to return to his Nevada mines.

He was privy to the most detailed information on the Comstock Lode, often weeks in advance of the announcement of a major strike, yet he refused to invest in the very stock market his money had created.

For many, the legend ends when, as the mines of Virginia City began to decline, he sold his remaining stocks and left Nevada, but it was really only a second beginning. Although he had once boasted to friends in a California gold camp that, if he ever managed to make $25,000, he would retire and "become a bum," he would make more than twenty-five million during his life and continue to work until the day he died.

In 1879, he invested half a million dollars in the development of a new explosive, many times more powerful than dynamite. When the Oakland, California, plant blew up the following year, he abandoned the investment and prepared to take a two-year vacation in Europe.

His vacation didn't last long. The Nevada legislature cabled MacKay that he had been named the state's representative at the Paris Exposition. More accolades followed. President Chester Arthur appointed him ambassador to the coronation of the first Russian czar, Alexander III.

MacKay returned to the United States frequently, content to leave his wife and children to make the rounds of the European social circles. Incensed by the cost of a trans-Atlantic cable (seventy-five cents a word!), he decided to start a cable company of his own. In partnership with James Gordon Bennet, he organized the Commercial Cable Company, laying cable across the treacherous Atlantic to London. Forced to contend with Western Union's refusal to relay his transmissions from London across the United States, MacKay began to buy up small, independent telegraph companies in America and soon had his system in operation.

Then another obstacle arose. Financier Jay Gould, who owned the existing trans-Atlantic company, dropped his rates from seventy-five to fifty cents a word. MacKay countered with forty cents; Gould followed suit. Soon there was a price war raging, and both men were losing money. Gould was incensed: "There is no beating John MacKay; if he needs another million or two he goes to his silver mine and digs it up." Apparently he was unaware that MacKay had sold his silver interests many years before.

In the end, both men emerged winners, agreeing on a standard rate of twenty-five cents a word. MacKay was free to oversee his new communications empire and give Western Union a run for the money.

When he died in 1902, the *New York Tribune* estimated his fortune at fifty million dollars. Other world publications guessed even higher. In response, his long-time friend and closest business associate, Dick Dey, commented, "I don't suppose he knew within twenty million what he was really worth."

Today a statue of MacKay stands on the University campus in Reno. Arm outstretched and pointing toward the distant Comstock Lode where he earned his vast wealth, MacKay is dressed, not in the clothes of a millionaire, but in the tattered shirt and pants of an underground miner. He would have approved. And while there are still fortunes to be made in Nevada, perhaps none will ever rival that of the legendary John MacKay.

The "Magnificent" Mrs. MacKay

Her collection of jewels was described as "the finest outside the royal treasuries." She sported a diamond bracelet that wrapped around her forearm, not once, but five times, and boasted more than 300 individual diamonds. For the princely sum of $300,000, she commissioned a necklace of diamonds and sapphires which became the rage of the Paris Exhibition of 1878. In all, her collection was estimated to be worth more than a million dollars, and that was well before the turn of the century. She once commissioned a French artist $15,440 to paint her portrait. But, she disliked it and had it burned.

She was Mrs. John MacKay, wife of the man who would become known as the King of the Comstock. During her lifetime, she became the darling of Paris, the toast of several continents. She spent more than three fortunes entertaining the elite of Europe. But who was this lady? And was her only real claim to fame the fact that she was married to a mining millionaire?

Marie Louise Hungerford was born in Brooklyn in 1843, the daughter of Daniel Hungerford, who had served with some distinction in the Mexican War. At the end of the war, Hungerford drifted to the gold camps of California. Upon his arrival in Downieville, he sent for his family, and they joined him on the mother lode. But the gold proved as elusive to Hungerford as to many other new arrivals. For the next several years, the family, which included daughter Marie and her younger sister, maintained a precarious existence. Hungerford took up barbering; his wife brought in washing to make ends meet.

Among the other gold seekers was a young physician, Edmund Bryant, a native New Yorker and cousin of the soon-to-be-famous poet, William Cullen Bryant. Though still in his early twenties, Bryant represented the best of what Downieville had to offer. Within a few months Bryant and young Marie Hungerford were married. By the time of the nuptials, word had reached California of the discovery of a gigantic vein of silver near a town called Virginia City in the Utah Territory. But the rumors of fabulous silver strikes were tempered with headlines of an Indian uprising in the region, and it would not be until the following year that the Bryants headed east. In 1861, the Hungerfords moved to Virginia City, and the newlywed Bryants moved to Steamboat Springs, in the shadow of Mount Davidson. There the doctor opened a health resort to take advantage of the hot springs that rose mysteriously from the earth. Two daughters, Eva and Marie, were born.

But Doctor Bryant fell victim to his own medicines. Helplessly addicted to a disastrous combination of alcohol and opium, the physician simply disappeared, leaving his wife and family on their own. Young Mrs. Bryant moved nearer to her father in Virginia City, where she taught French to the new well-to-do and took in sewing on the side. Her youngest daughter, Marie, fell ill and was buried in a silent grave overlooking the city.

Enter Mrs. James Fair, the wife of a wealthy mine owner. Mrs. Fair had been impressed with Marie Bryant's sewing abilities and worried constantly about the young woman's health. She began inviting the young mother to dinner, and it was there that Mrs. Fair, acting as matchmaker, introduced Marie to another mining magnate, John MacKay. The two were married at the Fair home. MacKay sent a case of champagne to all the newspapers, and the event made front page news along the Comstock. Marie was twenty-three, MacKay, thirty-six.

While the story up to this point sounds almost like a fairy tale, the marriage which followed seemed hardly so. Both MacKay and his young wife soon went their separate ways. Marie, perhaps in an attempt to compensate for her rather humble beginnings, basked in the limelight of high society and relished the lavish dinner parties and teas that her new-found wealth could provide. MacKay, on the other hand, preferred the company of hardrock miners and abhorred social events of any kind. He divided his time between his mining interests in Virginia City, which by now were yielding almost one million dollars a month, and his banking business in San Francisco. For much of the remainder of their lives they would live separately, she in utter splendor, he often in dilapidated hotel rooms. Yet the arrangement seemed to suit both amicably.

Marie MacKay's quest for respectability began immediately. First a new home was built on the slopes of Mount Davidson; within a year of its completion, she had selected a new residence, this time in San Francisco. By 1876, that home was abandoned as well. Marie MacKay, now with two young sons, John and Clarence, set off for

Europe. In Paris, she purchased a magnificent four-story mansion along the Champs-Elysees and immediately set out to redecorate it -- to the tune of a quarter of a million dollars. Now all that was needed were guests.

But it took more than money to break down the doors of European high society. For months, the frustrated Mrs. MacKay entertained no one more grandiose than her own United States ambassador. It would take a miracle to elevate her to the status which she so dearly sought. That miracle took the form of none other than Ulysses S. Grant, the Civil War hero fresh from four years in the White House. Grant was about to launch a triumphant world tour and would be in Paris for several days. If Grant could somehow be persuaded to stay at the MacKay mansion, his visit would, without doubt, open the doors to the crowned social heads of Europe....

An assist came from her father, Daniel Hungerford, who now was also living in Paris, his funds provided by a generous stipend from MacKay. Hungerford did not know Grant, but they both had served in the Mexican War. Hungerford wired an invitation to Grant, and the president accepted. Menus were engraved on sheets of pure Nevada silver. Although most of European society sniffed at the upstart woman from that barbarous place called Nevada, they clamored for invitations. The reception was the largest ever held in Paris; it was the most lavish event since Benjamin Franklin had visited the city a century before.

The event elevated Mrs. MacKay to a status she had only dreamed about. Her social status assured, Marie MacKay would remain in Europe for the next seventeen years, her only contact with her husband his infrequent visits to the continent. She returned to San Francisco briefly when she learned that he had been shot by an angry former business associate. By the time she had arrived, he had recovered, so she returned to Europe for another decade. When she finally crossed the Atlantic for the last time, it was to seal her husband's body in the family vault in Brooklyn.

Upon the death of her husband, Marie MacKay returned to an estate on Long Island. She lived there for more than twenty years, rarely venturing outside. She died in 1928, at the age of eighty-five. She had left her mark on this country and others. Of the fabulously rich individuals that America would produce throughout the coming years, the "magnificent" Mrs. MacKay was the first to use her fortunes to breach the shores of Europe. Europe would never be the same again.

The Newspaperman Was a Lady

Frontier newspapers were really something; they printed all the news that was fit to print and then some. Then, as now, it was considered just as important to keep the readers entertained as it was to keep them informed. On slow news days editors often "made up" the news, and few people actually seemed to care.

Mark Twain, during a stint as temporary editor of the *Territorial Enterprise*, wrote of the Empire City Massacre, a purely fictitious account of a brutal slaying of a pioneer family. Sam Davis, editor of the *Carson Daily Appeal*, went so far as to invent a rival newspaper, the *Wabuska Mangler*, against which he railed almost daily in an attempt to boost circulation. It was the longest running hoax in newspaper history. This creative journalism occasionally turned deadly. Dan DeQuille frequently had to "explain" some of his editorials at gunpoint, and a few times he was physically beaten. In 1874, a reporter for the *Daily Appeal* in Carson City actually took on a writer for the rival *Daily Tribune*, intent on settling their differences with six guns. Both men were wounded; one was crippled for life.

One of the most interesting series of events in the annals of frontier publishing began in 1892, when Anne Martin took over the state capital's afternoon paper, the *Carson News*. A tiny spinster, totally untrained in journalism, Martin had no publishing experience whatsoever, and history does not record how she came to that uncomfortable position. But that didn't keep her from making a valiant effort. She shrewdly decided that the only sure-fire way to keep subscriptions high was to create a sure-fire controversy. And so she did. Her eyes immediately fell on the rival *Daily Tribune*. She reasoned that if the two papers were to publicly battle it out, both would benefit. She was right.

The editorials began: first the *Tribune* would abuse both the *News* and Martin, in no uncertain terms; the *News* would counter with accusations of its own. The conflict continued for months, much to the delight of both the publications and their readers. But what was not generally known was that the controversy had been created entirely by Martin herself. The wily publisher, unable to write copy of her own, had actually hired the editor of the *Tribune*. Each day, that tall, courtly gentleman would enter her office, nod politely to Martin, and then proceed to an empty desk. There he would write the *News'* response to the very editorial that he had written for his own paper that same morning.

As ingenious at circulation as she was, Martin was also clever enough to take advantage of any opportunity that came her way. Throughout the 1800's, severe Sierra storms plagued the publishing business, and transportation difficulties frequently caused a shortage of paper. One such event brought to a head another feud, this time between Martin's *Carson News* and the *Carson Daily Appeal*, published by Sam Davis. Martin and Davis never missed a chance to criticize each other. In particular, whenever their paths happened to cross, each took the opportunity to upbraid the other for their touted circulation figures. Davis would claim preposterous numbers; Martin would call him a liar.

But one day the delivery of paper was halted, the result of bad weather or a trade embargo. In any event, there was a shortage of paper in the Carson Valley. Martin, again proving herself, while not a writer, at least an astute businesswoman, had a stockpile. Davis had none.

The publisher of the *Appeal* was eventually forced to approach his rival with hat in hand, begging to borrow at least enough paper to run off his next issue. Magnanimously, she consented, but on one condition: he would have to agree to take only as much as he needed to publish a single edition. Pledged to borrow only what he needed to print, the true circulation figures of the *Carson Appeal* quickly became evident. Revenge was sweet for Anne Martin. On the following day, she published the exact figures in her paper, proving that her own circulation was far greater, ending once and for all the rivalry between the two newspapers.

Anne Martin was the first female publisher in the Silver State and one of the very first in the entire country. Although she couldn't write and had no prior experience at the job, she still managed to issue a paper that was one of the most successful in the city. She published all the news that was fit to print and then some.

Tasker Oddie: Man of Reputation

It was the first good news to hit Nevada since the discovery of the Comstock. When Jim Butler's burros led him to what looked like a rich outcropping of ore, many were skeptical. But that had been four months earlier. Now the results were in: the find near what the Indians had been calling Tonopah was yielding unheard-of wealth. Men were selling meager shares in nearby claims for as much as $300,000. As it turned out, it was just the tip of the iceberg.

The news of the newest bonanza was spreading swiftly. Teamsters McLean and McSweeney rounded up 100 head of horses and mules in Mohave. With five wagons and trailers, they set out for Candeleria and Soda Springs for supplies. Almost overnight creature comforts sprang up in the barren desert. At the center of it all, of course, was Jim Butler, the man credited with locating the original find. But "Lazy Jim," as he was occasionally known, didn't have the cash on hand for an assay for his find. It would be his old partner, Tasker Oddie, not Butler, who learned the value of that strike. And Butler was not particularly interested in working his claims. He chose instead to oversee operations; the management of those claims went to Oddie. Besides cutting Oddie in on the deal, Butler had granted ore leases to more than 100 of his friends without even the scratch of a pen to define them. It was up to Oddie to keep Jim Butler from giving away the store.

Born in Brooklyn, New York, of a wealthy family, Tasker Lowndes Oddie had come west to seek his fortune in the mining camps of Nevada. He and Butler had been friends for years; he even replaced Butler as district attorney of Nye County. Oddie would eventually become rich beyond his wildest dreams. To some extent, he owed it all to Butler. Soon more than 1,000 horses and mules were hauling ore to the nearest railroad and on to the smelters. Of those shipments checked, recorded, and paid for by Tasker Oddie, there was never a single dispute. In the days of a quick buck and unscrupulous operators, it was an unusual friendship. The lucrative operation was based entirely on trust.

When Tasker Oddie became the brains behind the operation, he maintained an unsullied reputation for honesty. For example, Oddie had originally promised the assayer, a Mr. Gayhart, a small percentage for his services. When the total came in, the lucky assayer earned $31,500 for his work on but eight samples of ore. It set a record that has never been equalled.

Though a lawyer by trade and a miner only by avocation, Tasker Oddie soon became the first manager of the newly-formed Tonopah Mining Company.

But Oddie was not a man to sit behind a desk. He was a hands-on manager who was constantly in the field, as evidenced by a story related by Billy Metson, a mining camp lawyer, to author G.B. Glasscock: "One day I was taking a walk and just as I passed a big outcropping or 'blow out,' of rock thirty or forty feet high and probably a hundred feet long, I saw some men a little further east and north digging a hole. There were six or seven of them spelling one another and making the dirt fly pretty fast."

Lawyer Metson knew something was afoot. Under Nevada mining law, all that was necessary to secure a valid claim was to have a hole down ten feet. It was obvious that the men were attempting to jump the claim. What they didn't know was that the claim was represented by Tasker Oddie. Metson continued: "Almost immediately I saw Oddie running from the north towards the men. His idea was to block their sinking of the shaft to the required depth. I think the hole was from four to six feet deep. Oddie jumped right in the hole. Instantly guns came out. Oddie was unarmed but he was so intent upon defending his people's rights that he saw no other way to thwart the jumpers than to sacrifice himself by delaying the completion of their shaft."

Metson drew his revolver and leaped to Oddie's rescue. "My 'forty-five' probably looked ominous to the jumpers," he recalled, "for proceedings halted until some of the men who had followed Oddie arrived and took in the situation. They 'persuaded' the jumpers to leave."

But Metson was downplaying the gravity of the situation. The claimjumpers edged closer to their weapons. It was then that one of the men with Oddie stepped to the edge of the hole and said quietly, "This ground belongs to the Tonopah Mining Company; you'll have to get off."

"Who says so?" demanded their leader.

"I do," replied the tall newcomer.

"An' who the hell are you?" the claimjumper demanded.

"I'm Wyatt Earp," came the soft reply. The claimjumpers promptly beat a retreat.

Yes, Wyatt Earp had come to the aid of Tasker Oddie. Earp had become the most famous lawman in the west more than twenty-five years before when he, his brothers, Morgan and Virgil, and 'Doc' Holliday, had faced down the Clanton and McLaury brothers in the infamous gunfight at the O.K. Corral in Tombstone, Arizona. Earp, who was in the region to take over duties as a bouncer in the new Northern Saloon, needed little more than his reputation to settle the matter. The attempt to take over Oddie's claim had ended.

Tasker Oddie's reputation for honesty and fair play would serve him well. He would go on to prominence as Nevada's governor. After serving the term from 1911 to 1915, he was elected to the United States Senate in 1920 and once again in 1926.

But perhaps it never would have happened without the help of a lazy prospector by the name of Jim Butler and a man named Wyatt Earp. Thanks to them, Tasker Oddie, one of the founders of Tonopah, became quite a legend himself.

A District Attorney for Belmont

The good citizens of Belmont were outraged.

"I'm tired of the riff-raff taking over this town," said the owner of a small mercantile.

"Belmont is being bled dry!" exclaimed a banker.

"What we need is a man who can get something done!" cried the owner of an apothecary shop.

Indeed. Belmont was in a somewhat precarious position. In 1865, the region was populated by little more than a few starving jackrabbits. But by the following year there were more than 6,000 raucous miners swarming over the landscape. One particular mine, the Silver Bend, was allegedly yielding an incredible $100,000 a week in silver, all of it within a scant twenty-five feet of the surface.

But often the success of a boomtown depended on factors other than the richness of its ore. For investors to invest, for bankers to bank, and for the future to flourish, rules of order, by necessity, were required. It was imperative that law and order be established if a boomtown were to survive. So it was no wonder that the election of a new district attorney held such fascination for the residents of Nye County in the year 1892. In a small room in the rear of a Belmont assay office, a handful of the town's more prominent citizens had gathered to discuss the situation.

The leading candidate for the position was a schoolteacher by the name of Charles Deady, but Deady was hardly the aggressive, take-charge kind of guy envisioned by the town fathers. He had no legal experience, either. Said one of the politicos, "He has about as much appeal as Andy Johnson!"

A hush fell over the room. Andy Johnson, as everyone knew, was a mule rancher down along Mosquito Creek. Likeable, but totally uneducated, his only claim to fame was an illustrious handlebar mustache and a penchant for going weeks at a time without taking a bath. It was said that even sagebrush wilted when Andy passed by.

But mischief prevailed. When the suggestion was made to run Andy Johnson against Deady, all agreed. The plan was brilliant, they said. Obviously no one would vote for the old codger, but it sure would make folks think twice about voting for somebody like Deady. Fortified with several bottles of liquid inspiration, they set off for Johnson's dilapidated shack. Only one bottle was needed to convince the muleskinner that he was the only man for the job of district attorney for Nye County.

Of course, there is always one small problem with a practical joke: sometimes it backfires on you. To everyone's surprise and chagrin, Andy Johnson won the election handily. He was promptly sworn in as Nye County's district attorney.

Andy Johnson was certainly no politician, and he knew mules a whole lot better than he did people. But Johnson was smart enough to know he had to have help, so he enlisted the aid of a retired lawyer, William Granger. Granger agreed to serve as deputy district attorney and to handle all legal matters. To everyone's amazement, the two proved better than one. Andy Johnson was free to do his politicking, and Granger did most of the work. So effective was the duo that the legal affairs of Nye County were soon in tip-top shape. For four years, the pair made a credible accounting of themselves. Andy began to think he had a job for life.

But all good things must come to an end. In 1896, Belmont's political machine now threw its considerable weight against the man they had somehow elected just a few years before. They chose as their candidate a rancher from Monitor Valley, one Jim Butler. Butler, like Johnson before him, was uneducated and certainly no lawyer, but he was popular and was elected in a landslide.

Johnson was horrified. He would not honor the results, he said, and immediately demanded a recount of the vote. When the town fathers declined, Andy barricaded himself in his office, refusing to come out even for food. Stubbornly, he refused to open his doors unless a friendly face appeared with food or drink.

The town fathers were perplexed. Should they use force and storm the courthouse, or should they surround the building and try to starve Johnson out? It was a classic standoff.

In the end, Andy Johnson decided that perhaps life with his mules was preferable to a career at city hall. He finally turned over the keys to his office and retired to his ranch along Mosquito Creek.

And what of Jim Butler, the man who had won the office? Butler would preside as district attorney no more than a single term himself. Finding political life not to his liking, he was often gone weeks at a time, prospecting in the nearby hills. A short time later one of Butler's burros uncovered a ledge containing rich, silver-bearing ore. It would prove to be the largest strike since the days of the Comstock. The town of Tonopah sprang up, and former District Attorney Jim Butler became a very rich man.

Andy Johnson also made quite a fortune for himself. As more and more prospectors streamed into the region, his mules were suddenly bringing premium prices, and Andy began to enjoy his own prosperity.

Just goes to show you: nothing is stranger than politics -- especially in Nevada!

The Grand-Daddy of Them All

They named the site Grandpa, for they were convinced that the claim would become the richest in the state, the grand-daddy of them all. The two itinerant prospectors were right. Near that first claim would spring up perhaps the greatest boomtown central Nevada had ever known.

Billy Marsh and Harry Stimler were looking for a grubstake. The two had watched Tom Fisherman, a Shoshone Indian, work his magic with the tenderfeet in town, and they knew how to go about it. Old Tom had his routine down to a science. Not particularly interested in gold or silver himself, Tom nevertheless maintained an adequate supply of quartz-bearing rock for use whenever his whiskey supply ran low. Then Tom would single out a likely-looking prospect, and the exchange would go something like this:

Tenderfoot: "Where'd you get that rock?"

Tom: "Over there," and he would point a dirty finger off into the desert.

Tenderfoot: "Where? Could you find the place again?"

Tom: "Mebbe so. Need grubstake. You like this rock?"

And so it went. The stranger would study the rock again and again, trying not to appear too interested. Finally, he would offer Tom his grubstake, which usually took the old Indian no farther than the nearest saloon.

But Marsh and Stimler knew that once in a while old Tom actually did go prospecting. And, for some reason, he was extremely lucky. Hadn't he sold one claim west of Silver Peak for $5,000.00? The two men decided to test the Indian's skill.

First they went to none other than Jim Butler, the fellow who had made his fortune in the Tonopah strikes. Butler was willing to take a chance on the young prospectors, and he provided the two with a rickety buckboard, a double team consisting of one horse and a mule, some hay, and enough grub to get the party by for about a week. Two days later, led by the Shoshone, Marsh and Stimler reached Rabbit Springs. The next day, December 4, 1902, they climbed the slopes of what is today known as Columbia Mountain. There they found some good color, and they staked several claims. At once, with their "lucky" Indian in tow, they headed back to Tonopah with their samples.

The results were promising, but not as good as the two had anticipated. The bad news was that the samples proved to be worth only a little over twelve dollars a ton; the good news was that it was almost pure gold, the only such find ever recorded in the region. They christened their claim the Sandstorm and called the site Grandpa.

The rest, as they say, is history.

Word of the Marsh and Stimler find reached the ears of George Wingfield, later to become one of Nevada's most prominent businessmen. He offered the prospectors $1,000 for an option on the site, but the men were hesitant.

It was then that fate, quite literally, took a hand. While the two men were mulling over what appeared to be a generous offer, they happened to pass by the shop of a fortune teller who advised, "You own a rich mining claim. Someone wants to buy it from you. There is no need for you to worry. The option will not be taken up. The property will come back to you. Later you will sell it for a great deal more money than you are offered now." Marsh and Stimler took the advice. They allowed Wingfield his option.

Sure enough, the clairvoyant was right. Wingfield's option eventually lapsed, and the men found themselves once again in possession of the Sandstorm. In the meantime, however, a similar claim had sold for the incredible price of $10,000. The pair began to wonder if they had made the right decision.

Again, enter George Wingfield. This time he offered one of the partners, Harry Stimler, $1,000.00 for his interest. Stimler, who by now was thinking that he should take the money and run, teetered on the brink of indecision. After several days and a great deal of whiskey, he sold out to Wingfield. As was the case in a mining partnership where a man's word was his bond, he promptly turned over $500.00, or half his profit, to Billy Marsh.

Other strikes now popped up throughout the region. Gold fever spread like wildfire. Within several weeks a buyer offered the unbelievable sum of $25,000 to Marsh for the remaining interest in the Sandstorm. Marsh, who by now was finding the area too overpopulated for his liking, accepted. Again, with an incredible sense of fair play, he promptly turned over $12,500.00 to Harry Stimler.

Ironically one half of their claim had sold for $1,000 and the remaining half for over twenty times more. Still, both men were very happy to get it. Little did they know that they had been too hasty. Word of the strikes at Grandpa had spread clear across the nation. Within a month, with an influx of heavy equipment, the Sandstorm claim was worth more than one million dollars. But the fact that they had lost out on a fortune didn't seem to bother Marsh and Stimler. They had about $12,500.00 apiece; for men used to begging for their next grubstake, it was a small fortune.

Billy Marsh quit mining for good and invested his money in a little ranch near the town of Manhattan, providing hay and pack animals to the miners there. By 1930, he was still ranching, more than content with the cards that life had dealt. Harry Stimler was not so lucky. Twenty-eight years later, his fortune now depleted, Stimler was involved in a dispute with the postmaster of Tonopah, Nevada. The argument, over a borrowed rock crusher, was hardly worth the effort; Harry Stimler was shot and killed.

But Grandpa, the site that Marsh and Stimler had discovered, remains their legacy. And what a legacy it is. After the men sold out, someone decided that "Grandpa" just didn't do the town justice. They promptly changed the name of the place to Goldfield. It would go down in history as one of the richest finds in the Silver State.

Goldfield!

At the time of the first strike it was said, "Goldfield will go down in history as the Grandaddy of them all!" It was almost true. Miners flocked from as far away as Germany and Austria to be in on the excitement, and there was plenty. It was a raucous town, populated by determined men who had deserted other boomtowns before it. They came from places like Placerville, Virginia City, and Nome. Goldfield was born of hardship in a region known for desolation. For many of the prospectors, after having hit bottom elsewhere, there was a faint hope of a new beginning; it was also a new century. Still, back in 1902, the going was rough.

Mother Nature, always on the prod in Nevada, proved a particularly formidable opponent. The first winter taught many of the newcomers a quick lesson. At an altitude of 6,000 feet, the summit of the Saw Tooth Range got mighty chilly. A tent or dilapidated wood and tin shanty just wouldn't do. Temperatures dropped to thirty below, and the winds whipped along in freezing gusts up to forty miles an hour. For many of the miners, it was dig in or perish, and dig was exactly what they were forced to do. They began on the side of Coyote Wash. Laboriously, they dug horizontally back into the slopes, creating spacious caves. Next they hauled huge stones more than ten miles from Malapai Mesa to close off the openings and protect the caverns from the elements.

Surprisingly enough, the rude concept worked. The caves kept the first miners warm in the wintertime, quite cool in the summer. Blankets covering the floor and rudimentary furniture were sufficient for miners longing for the big bonanza. A few of those caves, the town's first real dwellings, survive to this day. They are still referred to by their majestic moniker, the Brownstone Mansions of Goldfield, so named for the colored rock that had been dragged up from the mesa.

Perhaps it was not a very auspicious beginning, but after that

153

first winter the future looked bright for Nevada's newest and richest boomtown. Within two short years, the name of Goldfield was known across the country. The caves were abandoned for high-rise brick buildings. Joining the usual assortment of saloons were banks, newspapers, churches, schools, brokerage houses, and businesses. Prize fights, the likes of which would rival any of those held in New York's Madison Square Garden, brought additional fame and fortune. Tex Rickard, the legendary promotor who had made his first fortune in the wilds of Alaska, brought top contenders to the city, and with them came the national press.

Rickard also opened the Northern Saloon which boasted "The Longest Bar in the West!", an amazing creation that was an incredible fifty feet long. In its heyday, service was provided by no less than two dozen bartenders at a time. The thriving establishment poured an average of six barrels of whiskey a day -- to say nothing of the vast amounts of beer and other beverages. Even the barber shops were "Goldfield-size." The Palace Shaving Parlour, operated by J.J. Noone, featured fourteen chairs and was heralded as the finest "west of the Mississippi and east of San Francisco!" By the end of 1905, Noone was using so much barbersoap that he would order it by the railroad car.

Even Wyatt Earp and his brother Virgil for a time called Goldfield home. Wyatt, who had bounced around the country for more than twenty years after establishing a reputation at the O.K. Corral in Tombstone, Arizona, found Goldfield to be "rich beyond belief." He promptly went to work for Rickard, overseeing the gambling tables for a small percentage and lending his famous name to the marque. So impressed was Wyatt that he wired his younger brother, Virgil, to come at once and eventually wangled him a job as well, first as a bouncer and later as a lawman.

But, as with many things too good to be true, the prosperity of Goldfield would soon end. In a few years, the miners went on strike. Within months, in 1907, a financial panic swept the nation. But for Goldfield, the worst was yet to come. In 1913, a freak cloudburst and subsequent flood destroyed much of what remained of her former glory. A decade later, when the town had dwindled in size to fewer than 5,000 people, a disastrous fire leveled the city. Its toll was twenty-seven city blocks. Finally, as if to mock the superstition that the third time is a charm, ten years later one of the worst blizzards of the century hit the area. Three terrible disasters, each ten years apart, marked the end of Goldfield's season in the sun.

Just the same, Goldfield left its mark not only upon Nevada but upon the nation as well. It made many rich, thousands secure for life. Wyatt Earp was not among them however. The famous marshall, hero of the most famous gunfight in the American west, left with little for greener pastures. Tonsorialist J.J. Noone closed his barber shop and moved on, eventually becoming a mortician. Only entrepreneur Rickard became famous; he parlayed his Goldfield success into a profitable career as a world-renowned boxing promotor. When he died, his body, encased in a casket made of solid bronze, lay in state in the middle of the arena in his beloved Madison Square Garden. More than 25,000 fans came to pay their respects.

Goldfield would not prove to be the granddaddy of them all as many had predicted, but it came pretty close. There would be other towns to make men rich though few would match Goldfield in its prime. Just the same, she served Nevada well -- bringing the Silver State into a new era just when many thought her riches had been tapped out.

I'll Take Manhattan...

Everyone knows about Manhattan: we bought the island from the Indians for some trinkets and beads, and then we threw up so many skyscrapers that you no longer can see the sky. But not too many people realize that Nevada has a Manhattan of its own, just about forty-five miles north of Tonopah. It never reached the world-renowned position of Manhattan, New York, but in its heyday it was quite a place, a place where a man could make a fortune with a little bit of luck and a generous dab of good old-fashioned frontier ingenuity. And you definitely could see plenty of sky.

The story is true. Our hero, if you can call him that, had left the east just a hop, skip, and a jump ahead of the law. It didn't take kindly to the way he was handling a notorious off-track betting operation, so George Graham Rice headed west. There, especially in the endless desolation of the Nevada desert, a man's credentials were rarely questioned. A good line and a hearty handshake were the stuff of which deals were made. And Rice was a dealer.

He had lost his $1,000 grubstake "bucking the tiger," the popular game of faro, in a Goldfield saloon; he was busted. When news reached him that a new discovery had been made in some remote, God-forsaken place called Manhattan, the destitute Rice wasted no time in pulling up stakes. "I was broke," he later recalled; "I bought blankets, a suit of canvas clothes lined with sheepskin and a folding iron cot, all on credit. I packed the outfit off to Tonopah and then climbed aboard a rickety old stage coach of the far-western type and started for Manhattan...a perilous journey that I would never again care to duplicate." He arrived in Manhattan with ten dollars -- borrowed -- to his name.

What he found that night was not inspiring to the seasoned con-man. Located at high altitude in a snow covered canyon, the camp appeared to be little more than a few huts and tents. He spent the night out in the open wrapped in blankets. But the following morning things looked a little better: "I strayed through the diggings. Sacks of ore in which gold was visible to the naked eye were piled on every side. The Stray Dog, the Jumping Jack and the Dexter were the three principal producers. They honeycombed one another. I questioned some of the prospectors as to the names of the single claims adjoining these and was informed that they could be bought for $5,000."

$5,000? How could a man with but ten dollars to his name get in on the action? George Graham Rice, eastern confidence man, instantly whipped out his checkbook. Of course he knew that he had no money in the bank; in fact, no bank in the west had even heard of him, but he was unconcerned. He was aware of something infinitely more important. Although he had been in town less than twenty-four hours, he knew Manhattan had no bank of its own. It would be weeks, perhaps even months, before anyone could verify his sad financial status.

What happened next epitomizes the way many unscrupulous speculators were able to amass sizeable fortunes in Nevada. Rice approached the owner of a likely looking claim and offered to pay the $5,000 asking price. Unfortunately, he explained, he had just arrived the previous day and had yet to have his funds transferred to the "fair city of Manhattan." Would the gentleman accept a $100 check drawn on the renowned Bank of San Francisco as an example of his good faith while he returned to the Bay city to retrieve his capital? The gentleman would. George Rice found himself with the deed to a promising claim. And he still had ten dollars in his pocket...

Though his story seemed quite plausible, Rice had no intention of going to San Francisco. Leaving his meager belongings behind, he quickly assembled some of the more promising samples from his claim and headed immediately for Goldfield. His first stop was the local bank. With the same winning smile, he managed to convince the wary banker that, should a check for $100 be presented in the near future, it must be honored. After all, he explained proudly, the name of George Graham Rice was renowned from coast to coast. He feigned indignity that the local banker was so uninformed. His bases now covered, Rice set out to make himself some real money.

He displayed his colorful specimens in the front window of a local jewelry store, explaining to the proprietor that they were "some of the richest in the world," and would be "a tremendous boom to your already thriving business." Again, the ruse worked. Soon, miners, speculators, and other confidence men were flocking to the jeweler's for a firsthand look. Wrote Rice later, "There was great excitement and before night a stampede from Goldfield to Manhattan ensued. Its magnitude surpassed even the first Goldfield rush."

George Rice followed his well-orchestrated rumor to Manhattan the following day. Although he expressed considerable reluctance to entertain offers to purchase his now-famous claim, he finally "succumbed" to the temptation. He sold his property for an incredible $20,000. He had parlayed his measly ten dollars into a sizeable fortune in less than a week. And he did it without even lifting a shovel.

The incident was typical of George Graham Rice. He continued to amass great fortunes throughout many of Nevada's mining camps -- and to lose them again. But he always managed to stay just one step ahead of the law. He even went on to write a book about his escapades entitled *My Adventures With Your Money*. George Graham Rice: confidence man extraordinaire.

How to Steal a Fortune

The year was 1904. The state's mining efforts had shifted from Virginia City and the slopes of Mount Davidson to the east, to places like Tonopah, Rawhide, and Goldfield. Into those towns came every sort of man imaginable, from card sharps and con men to grizzled prospectors, immigrant farmers, and high-faluting bankers. Not all of them struck it rich, of course. But as newer and bigger strikes were discovered, many men thought that the supply of gold and silver was virtually inexhaustible. Those who knew better shared the attitude of "Get your share quick, while the gettin's good!"

Often the methods of getting that share were decidedly larcenous. The most common practice was called high-grading. The concept was quite simple: if you couldn't find gold in your own mine, just help yourself to someone else's. Many did just that. It is estimated that, in the first year of operations at the Mohawk claim in the Goldfield area, more that $500,000 in ore was siphoned off by unscrupulous employees. Most men began by stealing just a tiny bit on a daily basis. After all, they reasoned, with so much of it lying around, it would hardly be missed. When enough ore was stashed away, they would take it to a "friendly" assayer who would be more than happy to convert it to cash -- for a fee, of course. Some assayers charged ten to fifteen percent of the value of the ore; some of the more greedy were able to glean as much as fifty percent for larger quantities.

Once the system was set in place, it was usually only a matter of time before the thefts became larger, more frequent, and even more ingenious. When the amount of stolen ore became too cumbersome to be carried away in a lunch bucket, most of the men resorted to wearing two shirts sewn together around the bottom. This hot and uncomfortable arrangement was soon refined into a heavy canvas jacket equipped with pockets all around, from the shoulders to the bottom hem. Worn under a regular work shirt, the jacket, called a "corset cover" by the miners, could hold up to seventy-five pounds of ore. So popular did they become that they were actually sold openly in supply stores!

One might wonder how a miner, loaded down with sometimes half his weight in ore, could manage to get by the watchful eye of a mine superintendent. In truth, these men often just looked the other way. Some miners actually paid for their jobs, as much as twenty dollars a day. With hundreds of men on the payroll, many superintendents made more in payoffs than the owners of the mines.

There are hundreds of stories about high-graders, and it is evident that the practice was openly tolerated. For example, Billy Cunningham, who operated the Oriental Saloon and Gambling Hall in Goldfield, recalled: "One miner deposited $1,133 in our safe over 8 successive shifts." Added Cunningham with a knowing look, "Pretty tough to do on $4.50 a day...." Still, no one ever bothered to report the miner to the authorities.

Some would say it would have been impossible to raise $150,000 on a miner's pay. But that amount of ore, pilfered from the Combination Mine, was found in the possession of three of the mine's own workers. In another incident, a U.S. Marshall arrested W.J. Langdon, a mining engineer, and an assayer, C.A. Pray, at Fallon, and confiscated a tool chest that contained ore worth in excess of $5,000. The lightness of their sentences indicates just how seriously the crime was considered: the two received a mere $500 fine or 100 days in jail. When it came to high-grading, the judicial system, like many mine superintendents, seemed to be looking the other way.

Assayers became wealthy men. With the opportunity to make up to fifty percent of the value of an ore sample, many assayers were setting up shop for the sole purpose of catering to high-graders. Within the first three years of Goldfield's existence, more than sixty assay shops had been set up, an open testimony to thievery. Natural exuberance and faith in the future of the region was so overwhelming that many thought high-grading was simply good advertising. After all, they reasoned, what could be better than telling the world you were so rich that even major theft was hardly enough to worry about?

The United States Geological Survey, an official government document published in 1909, had this to say about the rampant thefts that were occurring in central Nevada: "It is reported that miners in some cases refused $20.00 a day on development work in order to accept $5.00 a day with the opportunity for illegal prerequisites in the Mohawk [mine]. The extent to which high-grading went on during the year of 1906 is almost incredible!...It has been locally estimated that over $2,000,000 was stolen from the Mohawk, Red Top and Jumbo mines alone up to the later part of 1907."

Goldfield was wealthy, and Goldfield was booming. And if big money was being taken from the mines in the pockets of the workers, there was even bigger money coming in. Prominent national investors, men such as Charles Schwab, Bernard Baruch, and August Heinze, were investing. They brought a wealth of experience in railroads, finance, and politics, the essential ingredients of a sound future. With the influx of such men, Goldfield's mining industry cleaned up its act. Daily searches were conducted at the mines, and showers were required after the completion of a shift. The crooked assayers were invited to close up shop and move elsewhere. The practice of men paying for their jobs was abolished.

Goldfield, Nevada. For a time it was a hotbed of high-grading, a place of thieves and vagabonds, miners and millionaires. Nevertheless, it went on to establish its reputation as one of the richest boomtowns in the entire west.

Trouble in Goldfield

It was 1907, and George Wingfield, principal owner of the Goldfield Consolidated Mining Company, should have been a happy man. After all, his net worth now hovered somewhere near twenty million dollars, and his long-time partner, former banker George Nixon, had gone on to become a United States Senator, leaving George Wingfield the richest man in town. But trouble was brewing in Goldfield. And the trouble was "Big Bill" Haywood.

Haywood had gravitated to Goldfield from Butte, Montana. He was a tall man, well-built, and the patch he wore over one eye, the result of a childhood accident, gave him an somewhat ominous appearance. He had come to town as an organizer for the Industrial Workers of the World, or IWW, for short. The union, patterned after the teachings of Karl Marx, felt that the rich mines of Goldfield were ripe for unionization. But Goldfield's miners were already represented by the Goldfield Miners' Union. No problem, said "Big Bill," we'll simply create one large union to represent everyone, from miners to carpenters, from stone masons to hod carriers.

At first, the efforts of the IWW, which was dubbed the "I Won't Work" union, met with only passing interest and for good reason. Most of the miners were doing quite well all by themselves. Not only were they working for premium wages, but they were stealing enough each day to make most of the men wealthy. The process, called "high grading," was universally accepted, even taken for granted. Miners began by stuffing rich-looking pieces of rock into their pockets, then into their lunch boxes. They began wearing extra undershirts, sewn along the bottom hem with a draw-string inserted, forming a sort of sack under their regular shirts into which they could deposit even more. This creative garment was further refined into what were referred to as "corset covers," a fairly elaborate combination of pockets that allowed the miner to more comfortably remove even more gold-

165

bearing rock. The men were thus able to steal as much as fifty or sixty dollars a day -- in addition to their regular wages. These were indeed good times for the miners of Goldfield.

But George Wingfield vowed to put a stop to the high grading. At the entrance to each mine he set up a change room where the miner would disrobe and then walk naked into another room to put on his street clothes, all under the watchful eye of an armed guard.

His action caused tempers to flare. The miners now found their daily "income" threatened, and the IWW took up their fight with vigor. Those miners who refused to join the union were tarred and feathered, beaten mercilessly.

The situation escalated when L.C. Branson, owner of *The Goldfield Sun*, wrote a scathing editorial on the activities of the IWW. The union quickly retaliated, decreeing that no issues of the *Sun* would be sold. Venders were threatened with violence if they did not comply.

Enter George Wingfield -- with two guns strapped on his hips. He stormed into the newspaper office, gathering newsboys as he went, and bought out the entire edition. Next, he loaded each newsboy with all he could carry and told them all to get moving. With his two .44 calibers in plain sight, Wingfield walked the street, openly daring anyone to interfere. When no more papers could be sold, Wingfield gave the remaining newspapers away, leaving some at every saloon and store.

The incident precipitated the long-anticipated confrontation. Soon, many of the miners deserted the IWW and resurrected their original miners' union. But the IWW fought back. At the time, most miners were paid in script that was honored all over town. The IWW rallied support by demanding that the miners should be paid in cash and called for a major strike. They berated the mine owners, charging them with not valuing their labor enough to pay them in the coin of the realm.

Violence erupted. Fistfights in the streets were common, and there was a run on firearms in the city as the angry miners traded picks and shovels for rifles and shotguns. Suddenly, the prosperous town of Goldfield had become an armed camp. The tension continued to rise.

Things came to a head in December of 1907, when Wingfield called on his old friend, Senator George Nixon. He asked Nixon to appeal to President Roosevelt to send troops to Goldfield to prevent the spread of violence. Theodore Roosevelt complied. For the first and only time in the state's history, federal troops were on Nevada soil.

In later years, some would contend that the army was never actually needed, that George Wingfield, fearing the loss of power in

Goldfield, had simply called Nixon for support. Nonetheless, the arrival of government troops signaled the end of the trouble in Goldfield. In January, the Nevada legislature created the Nevada State Police; its first job was to relieve the federal troops. The trouble was over.

George Wingfield would go on to increase his fortune and to open the largest chain of banks in the state. Senator Nixon would die in office, and the town of Goldfield, like all boomtowns, eventually declined as the ore ran out.

And "Big Bill" Haywood, who had preached violence and a world-wide union? When he died in 1928, he was honored as a hero of the Soviet Union. His ashes were placed in the wall of the Kremlin, facing Red Square. Four lines in Russian praised his "courageous" work in the tiny mining town of Goldfield on behalf of Mother Russia.

The Man behind the Plank

"The cheapest and easiest way to become an influential man and be looked up to by the community at large was to stand behind a bar, wear a cluster-diamond pin, and sell whiskey."

Mark Twain said that, and he was experienced enough to know. He spent more time in saloons than half the residents of Virginia City, and when it came to drinking, the men of that fair city were certainly no slouches. The local saloon during the 1860's and 70's was a conglomeration of hotel, barbershop, bathhouse, and more, a place where preachers and politicians, painted women and prideful miners all held forth. It was unique to the American scene. But the saloon itself was only as important as the man behind the plank, for the bartender was one of any town's most vital citizens. He knew everything happening: the hold-ups, the shootouts, the births, the deaths, the illnesses. No politician could be elected without first currying the favor of the local mixologist. The local parson could not expect a full house without his help.

The bartenders were as varied as their establishments. Perhaps the most famous of Comstock wizards was Jeremiah Thomas, called by many "the Michelangelo of bartenders." So adept was he at mixing drinks that he designed and made his own bar tools. They were done in sterling silver, and they were worth $5,000 each. And that was at 1860's prices. "Customers called him 'professor,'" wrote author Richard Erdoes, and for good reason. "They tried to confound him with the fanciest orders imaginable but they never succeeded." Thomas is generally credited with creating the popular Tom and Jerry, conceived when a Virginia City miner demanded something that "would shake him down to the gizzard." Wrote Erdoes, "Ample-bellied, walrus mustachioed, with a lustrous jewel glittering on his stiff shirt button, dressed in an immaculate jacket of snowy white, he served up a bewildering variety of cobblers, slings, juleps, sours, sangarees, toddies and cocktails." And you thought all they drank in those days was red-eye.

And bartenders were showmen as well. Wrote Robert Pinkerton, "One particular barkeep was one of those oldtime experts who could slide glasses of beer along the bar and have each stop in front of the right customer. It was uncanny. The end of his bar was open, without a rail, and it was our favorite stunt to take a stranger there and have him stand at the end. The barkeep would shoot a full glass down swiftly. You'd think it was going right on thru the wall -- and the stranger was always sure of it. He'd duck and run, but the glass would stop four to six inches from the end, and nary a drop spilled."

In truth, however, few bars could boast a mixologist like Thomas. In the vast majority of saloons, the bartender just presented a bottle and a glass. The customer took as small or as large a drink as he pleased, in most cases the price ranging from ten to fifty cents. Good manners kept even the meanest drunk from filling his glass to the rim. Still, as one old cowboy remarked, "In them days we threw it down without a thing to chase it but the pleasant memory."

Near military posts, it was beer, not whiskey, which reigned supreme, mostly the result of army regulations and lucrative government contracts. On payday, at a small adobe saloon near Fort Churchill, business was so brisk that the bartender didn't even bother to draw the warm liquid. He merely dumped it into washtubs behind the bar and then dipped the glasses into the tubs as the occasion demanded. Not the most sanitary of conditions perhaps, but still greatly appreciated by thirsty troopers.

If you stepped into most saloons along the frontier and ordered something cold, you'd have identified yourself immediately as a tenderfoot. "It was sissified," wrote Erdoes. "There was never enough ice to keep milk from going sour and meat from going bad. [They] surely wouldn't waste the precious substance by throwing it in their likker. Besides," he added slyly, "it spoils the kick."

And the bartenders of old were generous to say the least. Some saloon keepers actually gave away more booze than they sold, the theory being that such largess was just another form of advertising which created a wealth of repeat business. Others, however, resorted to other means of making money. The following story from Virginia City is typical of how some saloon keepers could take advantage of unsuspecting travelers:

At Nevada I was called upon, shortly after my
arrival, by an athletic scarlet-faced man, who politely

said his name was Blaze.

'I have a little bill against you, sir,' he observed.

'A bill -- for what?'

'For drinks.'

'Drinks?'

'Yes sir, at my bar. I keep the well-known and highly respected coffee-house down the street.'

'But, my dear sir, there is a mistake. I never drank at your bar in my life.'

Replied the wily saloon man, 'I know it, sir. But that isn't the point. The point is this: I pay out money for good liquors, and it is the people's own fault if they don't drink them. There are the liquors -- do as you please about drinking them, but you must at least pay for them! Isn't that fair?

History doesn't record how the tenderfoot finally repled.

The man behind the plank -- he was truly one of the most important men on the frontier. He was a host, a psychiatrist, a preacher, a politician, and a friend. He was the first man a newcomer sought when he arrived on the scene and the last when it came time to leave. Wrote Mark Twain, "I am not sure but the saloon keeper held a shade higher rank than any other member of society." He was probably right.

171

A Tale of Two Cities

Although the twentieth century would dawn before Las Vegas became a city, its name is one of the oldest to be recorded in Nevada. The area, generally translated from Spanish as "The Meadows," provided a welcome respite for pioneers heading west. Its abundant streams and refreshing pools made an ideal resting place for settlers on the last leg of their torturous journey into the Mexican territory that was once Alta California.

It was Mormon pioneers who first decided to stay. Mormon leader Brigham Young had visualized a string of missions that would dot the route of the Old Spanish Trail. Once established, he viewed these missions as safe way stations for the Faithful who would disembark at Los Angeles and then make their way overland to the Mormon capital along the Great Salt Lake. He saw lush fields of grain and alfalfa, sprawling ranches overflowing with fattened beef. He even set in motion Nevada's first mining operation, a lead mine near Mount Potosi.

Although internal dissension among his early leaders forced abandonment of the first Las Vegas mission, from that time forth the city seemed to be one of true destiny. It would be more than half a century before Las Vegas would begin to grow again, but when it did, it would never look back.

The tale of this city begins with a murder...

In 1884, a ranchhand by the name of Hank Parrish shot and killed Arch Stewart, the owner of a neighboring ranch. Some speculated that the killing was justified -- that Stewart was difficult and overbearing. Parrish, however, had killed before. He had been arrested in an altercation resulting from a poker game in 1881; in 1890, he had been indicted for murder near the Lincoln County seat of Pioche.

But no matter. Arch Stewart was dead, and there was no

definitive proof of the murderer's identity. The widow Stewart enlisted the aid of ranch hands, fashioned a crude coffin, and quietly buried her husband in the desert. She had four small children at home and was pregnant with another, but this feisty woman wasn't ready to give up. She turned her small ranch house into a boardinghouse, a way station for hundreds of miners and prospectors who were heading out into the treacherous Nevada desert. According to Las Vegas historian Frank Wright, "No one passing through the Las Vegas Valley in the early days need go hungry or sleepless if Helen Stewart knew about them."

In 1902, events took a turn for the better for the widow Stewart. She sold part of her ranch to two men, men who would become bitter enemies. Each would vie for a city of his own in the midst of the barren southern Nevada desert.

A portion of the Stewart property went to a Canadian civil engineer, John McWilliams. The acreage, which today encompasses what is Washington and Bonanza streets, was divided into choice lots, and McWilliams felt his future was assured. Fifteen hundred people promptly moved into the area, and a freight station was built to house the dry goods, building materials, and other sundries that would eventually make their way to the new boomtown of Rhyolite. McWilliams proudly dubbed his new town the "Original Las Vegas Townsite."

But McWilliams didn't count on the business acumen of a Montana senator by the name of William Clark who had purchased another portion of the Stewart ranch. Clark also happened to be the principle owner of the San Pedro, Los Angeles and Salt Lake Railroad, the line that would be the vital link in the development of the southwestern United States. Clark immediately put plans of his own into play.

Clark built a railroad station on his property and decided to subsidize the remainder, about 900 acres, located on the east side of the tracks. That property, which today includes Main, Stewart, Clark, and Fifth Streets, would be offered for sale as well. Clark's advantage included his own railroad, a powerful force in the southwest. Though both he and McWilliams advertised extensively in Los Angeles newspapers, it would be Clark's railroad that would bring the eager buyers to the spot. William Clark literally had managed to obtain a captive audience of investors.

But with the shrewdness of a modern Wall Street financier, Clark added another, more dramatic twist to the rush to buy land. Once the prospective buyers had arrived, he noted that would-be purchasers outnumbered his lots by a substantial margin. He wisely postponed his sale to whet the anxious appetites still further. Then, he proudly announced that no sale would be held at all; it would be an auction instead, with the "valuable" property going only to the highest bidder.

It worked. On May 15, 1905, in 110 degree heat, many of Clark's lots brought four times their original value. Most were snapped up before the day's end. The raucous land sale spelled the end of McWilliams' hopes. Even the building which housed the local newspaper, the *Las Vegas Age*, was jacked up and moved to the Clark side of the railroad tracks.

So ends the tale of two cities. Las Vegas now was a single entity, a town that would grow beyond the hopes and dreams of even the clever William Clark.

Making a New County

Back in 1864, the year of Nevada's birth as a state, creating a county was a simple matter of following the basic laws of nature, to follow the paths of rivers, ridges, and streams. As to the matter of the county seat, that was most often determined by which settlement was the richest, or claimed to be. To create a county seat, you bought it, and therein lies a tale...

Lincoln County, named patriotically for Nevada's favorite President, Abraham Lincoln, was a case in point. It was spread precariously over more than 18,500 square miles, an area large enough to hold several eastern states in their entirety. At the time, the center of the action in Lincoln was the boomtown of Pioche, a rough and tumble mining camp. Pioche was rich; gold and silver claims dotted the landscape like chuckholes on the prairie. A bright future was predicted for Lincoln County and for Pioche, its most prosperous city.

So, it seemed logical that in 1866, two scant years after Nevada's statehood had been declared, the Nevada Legislature did not hesitate in selecting Pioche as the Lincoln County seat. It mattered little that most of the county lay to the south, for it was unpopulated, the home of a few ranches and a few roving bands of Shoshone and Paiutes. Even dedicated and determined Mormon pioneers had forsaken what would be the southern portion of Lincoln years earlier. One of the faithful muttered, "There is nothing here to eat but lizards."

But boomtowns go bust with frightening regularity, and Pioche was no exception. Miners and prospectors, speculators and stock manipulators eventually moved on to a place called Searchlight, 460 tortuous miles to the south, and by the turn of the century, the face of the Lincoln County had changed. Pioche was still a viable population center; in fact, it had gone into debt to construct a fabulous new county courthouse. But Searchlight was booming, and now another place to the south, a small railhead known as Las Vegas, had begun to grow.

Pioche found itself seriously in debt, with no prospects of repayment, and folks in Lincoln County found themselves with a monumental problem on their hands.

On the surface, the solution seemed simple enough: move the county seat to Searchlight. But doomsayers warned that Searchlight could soon go the way of Pioche, from boom to borrasca in an instant. More seasoned residents suggested Las Vegas as a logical alternative. After all, Las Vegas had the San Pedro, Los Angeles and Salt Lake Railroad, and railroads, as everyone knew, were the key to long-term western expansion.

Pioche, of course, would have none of it. Pioche was the county seat, and the county seat it would remain. But by 1905, the situation had worsened. Pioche was now more than $630,000 in debt, and county lawmakers were noisily bemoaning the fact that the journey to a dying city in the north was hardly worth the time and effort. They called long and loudly for relocation of the county seat.

It would be the fledgling rail city of Las Vegas that would take the initiative. In 1908, the Lincoln County Division Club was formed. Instead of simply moving the county seat, they reasoned, why not create an entirely new county? After all, Lincoln was certainly big enough. And wasn't Las Vegas itself fast overtaking Searchlight as the largest city in the region? Voters lined up to enter the fray.

A heated election that year featured a race for the office of county treasurer. On one side, Henry Lee, a northern resident, vehemently opposed splitting the county; on the other, pro-division incumbent Ed Clark led the forces for a new county. Lee won the election. His first official act was to remove all county funds from the Las Vegas area and place them in the "safety" of the Bank of Pioche. That move would turn out to be the straw that broke the camel's back.

Though Clark had lost his bid for re-election as county treasurer, most of the other elected positions were won by pro-division forces. Heavily armed with both petitions and patriotism, Las Vegas officials deluged the state legislature with overwhelming confidence in their cause. On July 1, 1909, Governor Denver Dickerson signed into law a bill creating Clark County out of Lincoln. When money was pledged with which to build a new court house, the die was cast. There was a brand new county and a new county seat. The city of Las Vegas had finally come into its own.

Ironically, the city, which today is the richest in the state, began its first year almost as heavily in debt as Pioche. As historian Frank Wright reports, "County debt was divided too, based on the new and old counties' assets. Richer than her older, northern neighbor, Clark County started life $430,000 in the red!"

Eventually, however, would come the Boulder Canyon Project, the largest construction endeavor of its time. The result was the creation of a monumental structure now known as Hoover Dam. Las Vegas turned red into black. The city and its county would never look back.

The Last Stagecoach Robbery

Just south of the Idaho border, the jagged walls of Jarbidge Canyon slice fifteen miles into Nevada. Along the canyon floor flows the churning Jarbidge River. Gold was discovered here, and a mining camp was born. Jarbidge is a Shoshone word meaning "evil spirit." The name is apt, for there was evil lurking in the canyon that day.

It was December 5, 1916. High winds and drifting snows had made the trail almost impassable by the time the stagecoach carrying the mail and $4,000 in coin reached the top of the Crippen Grade. Below was the town of Jarbidge. The narrow road, with treacherous drop-offs, was nearly obliterated by the falling snow, and the driver, thirty-year-old Fred Searcy, fought constantly to keep the stagecoach from plummeting over the edge of the grade. He shivered in the cold, his gloved hands nearly frozen into claws, his eyebrows and lashes caked with frost. He was exhausted. He shifted his foot against the mail pouch beneath his seat as if to assure himself it was still there. He was running late and wondered whether the miners, anxious to cash their paychecks, were getting worried. But the end of the journey was close at hand; soon he would arrive in Jarbidge, pour himself a double whiskey and sit by the nearest stove. With these comforting thoughts in mind, he snapped the reins of his team, and the animals picked up speed.

As evening blanketed the area in darkness, Mrs. Dexter, who lived in a small house on the outskirts of the mining camp, looked up from her sewing at the sound of a shot. Someone shooting coyotes, she mused. But her thoughts had drifted elsewhere by the time the stagecoach passed by. Though Mrs. Dexter could barely see through the blinding snow, she knew Fred Searcy had finally made it into town with the mine payroll and phoned Postmaster John Fleming with the good news. But four hours later there was still no sign of Searcy or his coach. Postmaster Fleming alerted the authorities.

A search party was quickly formed, and more than thirty men set out into the snowstorm. After an hour, the freezing night air forced some of the men to abandon the search, but a few trudged on into the darkness. Fred Searcy and his coach had to be somewhere along the road, but where? It was Neale Hendryx, a prospector, who first spotted the tracks that veered off the road onto an old trail no longer used. In a clump of willows several hundred yards from the main street, the missing stagecoach was found, shrouded with snow. But not even the blanket of white could obliterate the form slumped over the driver's seat. Fred Searcy had been shot once in the head.

Spreading out, the search party quickly located several second-class mail sacks. They had been slit open, and bloodstained envelopes were scattered on the ground, their contents strewn about. But the first-class sacks, the ones containing the long-awaited payroll, were gone. Nothing more remained than a few rapidly disappearing footprints. Then the searchers came across prints that seemed to have been made by a dog...

The next morning the searchers set out to find the mysterious canine. They checked scores of animals before a big yellow dog was taken to the murder scene. The animal began digging furiously in the snow and uncovered a first-class mail pouch with a bloody handprint. The money was gone, but there were several letters, including one with a bloody thumbprint on it. The miners of Jarbidge had their first real clue to Searcy's murderer.

Witnesses identified the dog as a stray befriended by a man named Ben Kuhl. Thirty-three years old, Kuhl had come to Jarbidge as a cook for the miners, and he ran with a rough crowd. Among them were Ed Beck, a part-time miner, Cut-Lip Swede, a full-time drunk, and Billy McGraw, a miner with an indifferent attitude toward work.

A hasty search of Ben Kuhl's cabin uncovered a .45 caliber revolver, recently fired. A single shell was missing. When the sheriff arrived on the scene, he was met by the justice of the peace and a witness, of sorts -- a big, shaggy, yellow dog. Ben Kuhl was taken into custody.

In the fall of 1917, a trial was held in Elko, Nevada. The case for the prosecution was airtight. As the crime was recreated, the evidence against Kuhl was ominously clear. Someone had slipped out of town on Wednesday afternoon and climbed a hillside overlooking the road to Jarbidge. As the stagecoach approached, the killer leaped aboard and shot the driver. This was the shot that Mrs. Dexter had heard. The man who had driven past her house was not Fred Searcy but his murderer. It could have been the perfect crime. Until, that is, a dog led authorities to Ben Kuhl.

During the trial, Kuhl tried unsuccessfully to throw blame on his friends Beck, Cut-Lip Swede, and McGraw, but to no avail. He claimed at first that the gun was not his, that he had loaned it out. He claimed that he has been nowhere near the roadway that night, that he had been drinking with friends. Those friends, however, failed to come forward.

Although Kuhl pleaded innocent, it was a new twist in criminal identification that would prove to be his undoing. The prosecution introduced into evidence the mail pouch with the bloody handprint. Experts convinced the jury that the handprint had been made by Kuhl. It was the first time such identification was allowed in a United States courtroom.

On October 6, 1917, Ben Kuhl was found guilty of first degree murder and sentenced to death. He appealed to the Nevada Supreme Court, but the opinion, written by Justice Pat McCarran, upheld the conviction, citing the bloody handprint.

As the date of his execution approached, Kuhl finally confessed. He claimed that the driver, Fred Searcy, was going to help him fake the hold-up, that Searcy had changed his mind, that the two had struggled for the gun, and Searcy had been killed accidentally. Although the court didn't believe him, it converted his sentence to life. Ben Kuhl was transferred to the Nevada State Prison where he spent the next twenty-six years in maximum security, turned down for parole a record twenty-seven times. In 1944, sixty and terminally ill, Kuhl was released and died in Sacramento six months later.

The big yellow dog that led lawmen to the murderer? History lends no clue to its fate, but it's doubtful that Kuhl remembered him as "man's best friend." And the gold? It was never recovered. Some say it still lies buried in the rugged terrain near Jarbidge, $4,000 in sparkling gold coins. And many native Americans still believe that an evil spirit dwells in the region, and it could be true. But the robbery of the stage to Jarbidge continues to live on in Nevada's history, for it was the last stagecoach robbery in the United States.

Wild Horse Kitty: Queen of Diamonds

At one time the West was a land of sprawling ranches and open prairies. From Texas to Montana, from Idaho to the Oregon border, the millions of acres of unfenced land and the colorful life of the American cowboy was the stuff from which legends are made. We have had fictional heroes such as Owen Wister's Virginian, who stared down danger with a smile, the larger-than-life characters created by Randolph Scott and John Wayne, and the real-life cowboys, men like John Chism and Charlie Goodnight, who blazed dusty trails that still remain to this day.

But when we think back to those times from which the legends have sprung, few women come to mind. Although there in great numbers, they are usually thought of as secondary characters, leading tedious, dull lives, relegated to the background, cooking, washing, and raising the youngsters, ready to bathe the bullet wounds of the hero, and cure the fevers of the men who "really" won the west. Failing that, their role is one of the spinster-like school marm or the lowly prostitute. In reality, they were taming the land, helping the towns grow right along with the men. There are many examples to dispel the myth of nonentity, and Laura Wilkins is a perfect, yet little-known example.

Most people knew her simply as "Kitty." In her lifetime, Wilkins ran one of the largest ranching operations in the entire country, boasted one of the largest horse herds to ever roam the American continent, and trained some of the finest cowhands the west had ever seen. Kitty Wilkins was hardly the usual female stereotype.

An only daughter, she was born in Ogden, Utah. As a youngster, she became an accomplished pianist and took great delight in entertaining visitors with her virtuosity. When she was still a small child, the family moved to Tuscarora, Nevada, where, in the midst of the short-lived mining boom, her parents operated a small but prosperous hotel. When a disastrous fire consumed much of the town in 1879, the family moved to the Bruneau Valley and began a ranch. From there young Kitty would never look back.

From early childhood, Kitty Wilkins had been an accomplished rider, used to the ways of the range and comfortable around the hardened men who called it home. The area near Jarbidge, in Elko County, had yet to experience the rush of miners, and few people realized that the valley was home to one of the largest herds of wild horses in the country.

The fleet-footed animals, descendants of those brought by Spanish explorers, had ranged freely over much of northern Nevada and southwestern Idaho for more than a century. Those that had been captured by Indians were never castrated and continued to multiply unchecked. These mustangs Kitty encountered were incredible animals. They could smell water from five miles away, were strong enough to run great distances without tiring, rugged enough to negotiate the treacherous foothills and barren desert.

As the herds grew, the bands of wild mustangs began to threaten the cattle ranches that had sprung up in the region. Wild stallions would lure mares from corrals; entire herds would take over a grassy plain and literally pull the grass out by the roots, ruining it forever for cattle grazing. For Kitty, this presented a golden opportunity. If she could capture some of these horses, perhaps she could build a herd of her own. She wasted no time in forming a partnership with her brother, John.

Kitty Wilkins, riding side-saddle with her men through the rugged country, began a round-up the likes of which had rarely been seen in the territory. She hired only the best riders and cowhands, including Jess Coates, a Nevada cowboy who would eventually give a command performance before the King and Queen of England, Walter "Death Valley" Scotty, and Hugo Strickland, the nation's World Champion bronc buster. Soon, her initial herd had grown from a few dozen horses to more than a thousand.

She expanded her operation. She traveled east where her formal education and big-city refinement enabled her to land lucrative contracts with the United States government. She set up a pilot program which successfully bred wild mustangs with the best of her own herd. Soon the Diamond, her personal brand, became known throughout the west. By the turn of the century, no less than 20,000 horses wore the mark of the Diamond. From the giant stockyards of Chicago and Kansas City, to the luxurious theaters of San Francisco, Kitty was toasted as the "Queen of Diamonds." Kitty Wilkins had built one of the largest horse operations in the history of the great

American West.

But civilization was slowly creeping in, even to the far regions of Elko County. In 1910, Kitty's Hot Hole, site of a hot spring that bubbled out of the ground and into the East Fork River, became the subject of a lawsuit. When gold was discovered at Jarbidge, one C.C. Logan claimed squatter's rights on what was some of Kitty's best grazing land, contending that the property was now too valuable to be left to wild mustangs. It was the beginning of the end for the wild horse and wild horse ranches in Nevada.

By the end of World War I, most of the good range land was gone, as were the horse markets. Smaller ranches, fueled by vast irrigation projects, saw fences appear across the endless range. The automobile soon became the accepted mode of transportation. Within a few years, the hardy mustangs, now believed to be a menace to a more civilized way of life, were hunted and slaughtered unmercifully, often with the help of a new-fangled machine called the airplane.

By 1919, Kitty Wilkins had sold her ranches and her beloved horses and retired to a home in Glensferry, Idaho, where she remained until her death in 1936. Although she is little remembered today, Kitty Wilkins, the Queen of Diamonds, is truly a legend of the American West.

Old Newspapers Never Die

"Better Than Gold Is A Thinking Mind!" So proclaimed the masthead of a little-known Nevada newspaper, the *Pine Grove Burlesque*. It was little-known because it only published one copy of a single issue. That copy was kept on the counter of a general store solely for the convenience of its customers. Jake Highton has chronicled the history of publication in the Silver State in *Nevada Newspaper Days*; the story of the *Burlesque* is detailed there.

Despite its very limited circulation, the *Burlesque* did what modern newspapers often fail to do: it made its readers laugh, deliberately. How long has it been since you've looked up from your morning paper and let go with a loud guffaw that was intentionally prompted by the newspaper?

The *Burlesque* was typical of many early frontier publications. It was written almost entirely tongue-in-cheek, primarily for the benefit of a small number of local residents. Nothing was sacred, not even the ads for the newspaper's own employees: "WANTED at the *Burlesque* office: an able-bodied, hard-working, bad-tempered, not-to-be-put-off, and not to be backed down, freckled face young man to collect for this paper. He must furnish his own horse, pistols, Bowie knife, whiskey, cowhide, etc. We will furnish the accounts and we promise such a young man consistent and laborious employment." As if to emphasize the precariousness of publishing in early Nevada, the editor added, "But he must not expect any pay until he collects it from the subscribers."

Some early Nevada papers were actually written in longhand. The *Granite Times*, "Devoted to the Mining and Material Interests of Granite and the Mountain View District," was just such a paper. Its headlines were done in blue pencil, and the stories were done in longhand. Even so, the paper wasn't exactly cheap. Each edition cost one dollar, an exorbitant price for the times. A special Easter Sunday edition, even with its longhand method of reporting, brought five dollars. Proof-reading, however, left a lot to be desired. This headline appeared in 1908: "Graite To Have Cheaper Water!" The "n" in "Granite" had disappeared.

The *Silver Bow Standard* hardly set records for journalistic excellence, but it did set one for being, at least on one occasion, the most expensive newspaper ever produced -- its headline was printed in gold dust! The headline, which stated proudly and in no uncertain terms, "The Blue Horse Is A Great Mine!" was printed, according to the editor, in ink mixed with gold dust that assayed out at $80,000 a ton...

If early headlines were impressive, the copy itself was particularly so. Early journalistic prose was often flowery, almost poetic in its content. This account of a disastrous fire which almost destroyed the mining town of Eureka appeared in the *Eureka Sentinel*: "No more thrilling spectacle could be witnessed than when the fire was at its height, and the seething, roaring flames were carried along at almost lightning speed by the hurricane. No more beautiful sight was ever seen than when the fire climbed the mountainside and communicated to the sage brush. The mountain looked as though it was dotted by campfires."

Most Nevada towns boasted more than one newspaper, and they often disagreed. For example, the Eureka *Daily Leader*, competitor of the *Sentinel*, had an entirely different view of the same conflagration, and the *Leader* did not find the fire "beautiful" in the least: "A vast multitude of people, frantic with excitement, crazy with fear, and almost insane by reason of their losses, were running to and fro in an endeavor to save something from the general wreck. Half clad women, haggard and pale, weeping, shrieking, imploring help...."

Most Nevada newspapers came and went with the frequency of the camps that they had hastened to serve. As a mining town went bust, most editors simply ordered up a few wagons, loaded their press and type, and followed the hoard of prospectors to the next town. There they set up shop again under a different name. But as fleeting as such enterprises were, the closing of a frontier newspaper was a sad affair. Most papers were small, mom-and-pop operations, truly a labor of love for their editors. The demise of *The Oasis*, published weekly for the residents of Hawthorne by Orlando E. Jones, was a case in point. "This is a world of sadness," wrote Jones in his final editorial; "It becomes the sad duty of the undersigned to announce that with this issue his connection with *The Oasis*, either as editor or manager, ceases. The enterprise started as an experiment, and the experiment is a failure." Jones went on to explain the harsh financial realities associated with the newspaper business:

> It may be possible to publish a newspaper on
> one square meal a week; but to undertake to do so on
> one square a month, and hash only once in thirty-one
> days for the long months, is a little more than human
> nature can stand. It might be done in Missouri but it
> will prove a dead failure every time in Nevada.
> Hawthorne has a future before it, and we look for the
> building up of an inland town of considerable
> importance. But printers, as a rule are not wealthy
> enough to run a paper for glory. To those friends who
> have endeavored to aid the enterprise by patronage
> and encouragement, we return our sincere thanks.
> Liberty and Nevada. Ta ta.

Edward Niles, who put out the *Carson Times*, was another
editor who learned just how precarious frontier publishing was. On
July 11, 1881, he sent a printed index card to each of his former
subscribers with the following inscription:

> I started this business with limited capital and
> incurred a debt of $2,500 for press, type and necessary
> outfit. Payments fell due recently....Conscious of
> having ministered faithfully to a generous army of
> advertisers; a valued corps of subscribers and a
> cheerful squad of deadheads -- and also with the belief
> that the TIMES has been lively, enterprising and
> moderately entertaining; its editor and publisher bears
> malice toward none, and all that sort of thing and will
> soon enter a new field of labor, trusting at some future
> time to profit by experience and with ample capital to
> again enter the editorial ranks.

Frontier newspapers were humorous, lively, often newsworthy
in themselves. They were the very heart and soul of the early west.

She Was Just a Frontier Doctor

Because I am a native American and citizen of the United States, but do not feel like one unless I have the rights and privileges of the masculine citizen...

Because taxation without representation is tyranny in the case of women as well as men...

Because no citizen can represent another at the polls. If he can, why not vote by proxy?

Because being a woman, I can see things from a woman's viewpoint. Hence, no man, however willing he may be to suppress his own view in my behalf, could represent me at the ballot box or anywhere else...

Because man cannot fill woman's place in the economy of nature, nor in socio-economy. How then can he fill her place in the political economy of the nation?

Because I believe women fully as capable if assisting in the government of the home, though I have heard until I am tired that women cannot fight, and therefore should not vote, I still believe that when men are on the battlefield they cannot be at home and consequently, women have to do their work and that of a man.

Because I, an adult American woman, am opposed to being placed politically on par with the convict, the insane, the   idiot, the Indian and the minor, and below the ignorant foreigner who cannot read or write his own name...

Because if the right to vote is the evidence of a man's freedom and citizenship, the absence of that right shows that woman is neither free nor a citizen...

Because I believe in justice for all, and feel that there is no justice in denying the ballot to one-half of humanity because of a difference of physical confirmation, since there can be no doubt that man, with the same mentality as woman would be allowed to vote as the lowest specimen of the masculine gender, rather the exceptions noted are allowed a voice in the affairs of our government...

Because I believe in the natural equality of the sexes before the laws, political, social and moral...

That credo was written in 1894, when the women's rights movement was scarcely getting off the ground. At that time, anyone espousing its message, male or female, ran the very real risk of being drummed out of the territory. But the woman who wrote those stirring lines was not to be taken lightly, for she had beaten the odds before. She was Eliza Cook, the first woman doctor in Nevada.

Eliza Cook was born in Salt Lake City, Utah, in 1856. Little is known of her father, but young Eliza, her mother, and her sister moved to the Carson Valley in 1870. After a long illness, her mother died, leaving the two sisters in the care of an uncle. But Eliza Cook was not one to rely on the charity of others, and although there were many offers, she refused to take a husband. Instead she went to work for Dr. H. H. Smith in the small ranching community of Genoa. Smith was so impressed with the young woman that he encouraged her to take up the study of medicine herself. This was a bold undertaking at the time, for women who attended medical schools were ostracized, required to sit behind curtains, separated, preferably neither seen nor heard. But within two years, Cook had received her degree from Cooper School of Medicine, forerunner of Stanford University. At the age of twenty-eight, Eliza Cook began a frontier practice that would last almost half a century.

The work was demanding; days often lasted a grueling twenty hours. Doctors were few and far between in the sprawling valley and so were in constant demand. Isolated ranches, sometimes located more than forty miles away, often reached by non-existent roads, made travel in her buckboard an adventure in itself. The weather, which ranged from blazing summer heat to freezing winter cold made travel hazardous at best.

But none of this deterred Eliza Cook. Old photographs show her to be tall and slender, an attractive woman who dressed simply but elegantly, fond of long black dresses with high collars. She knew most of her patients by their first names. They, in turn, reverently referred to her as "Auntie."

Auntie Cook's practice thrived, as much a result of her personal touch as of her professional skills. She baked cookies for sick youngsters, brought home-made preserves, cakes, pies, and apple butter to ranchers. Cut off from the luxury of a pharmacy in Genoa, she dispensed the drugs herself, often measuring out prescriptions in sterilized bits of tissue paper. "She was extremely well-read and travelled extensively during her lifetime," wrote author Anne Seagraves; "She gave frequent lectures and was a respected speaker as well as dedicated doctor."

By 1894, Cook had taken another daring step. She joined the women's suffrage movement, began circulating petitions and lecturing against the "bondage" of Nevada women. From isolated ranches and farms, from cities, even from railroad cars, they came. Whenever Eliza Cook appeared, women flocked to hear her speak. Men, impressed by her courage and professionalism as a physician, attended as well. It would be almost three decades before the 19th Amendment, giving women the right to vote, was passed in 1920. Nonetheless, Eliza Cook had become Nevada's foremost spokesperson for women's rights.

While she continued to labor for the suffrage movement, she kept up her grueling practice as well. In later years, she traded her horse and buggy for a Model T, but her caring ways and gentle manner remained the same. She eventually retired from active practice shortly after the 19th Amendment was passed. She never married and chose to remain in the Carson Valley. In 1947, at the age of 91, Eliza Cook passed away quietly in her sleep, a true pioneer to the very end.

Accolades have been numerous for this amazing pioneer, but perhaps her most fitting tribute is this: today many of the babies that she delivered are leading citizens of the valley that she called home. These men and women, her true legacy, still remember fondly the first woman doctor in Nevada.

Sin and Perdition in Nevada!

The United Presbyterians of California sent their condolences, extending "sympathy to our fellow Christians who must live and labor to promote morality in Nevada under the unhappy handicap which the moral breakdown of the state presents." The *Chicago Tribune* called for a repeal of Nevada's statehood. President Harry Truman would later assert in his personal diary that Nevada would become "hell on earth," and called the state "a disgrace to free government."

What was all the fuss? Quite simply, Nevada had done the unthinkable in the eyes of much of the country: it had legalized gambling. On that day in 1931, few in Nevada thought the new gambling law more than a tempest in a teapot. After all, gambling had been allowed on and off since 1864, and even in areas where it was prohibited, most officials simply looked the other way. Still, community leaders like Anne Martin, Nevada's first women's rights leader, had been railing against the evils of gambling for years.

Wrote Martin in 1922, "A characteristic Nevada sight, and to those who know its significance one of the most pathetic, is the large groups of roughly dressed men aimlessly wandering about the streets or standing on the street corners of Reno, Lovelock, Winnemucca, Battle Mountain, Elko, Wells, Ely, Tonopah, Goldfield and other towns, every day in the year. They are in from the ranches and mines for the holiday with hard-earned money and the only place they have to spend it is in the numerous men's lodging houses, gambling dens, or brothels."

While Martin was right -- there truly was little recreation in Nevada at the time -- her description lost sight of the serious economic problems that had befallen the state. According to author Jerome Edwards, Nevada's entire state-wide population was less than that of Camden, New Jersey, with one resident per square mile. Nevada's mines had begun to falter, and there was no new industry, crop, or

197

service lingering in the wings. Nevada was in the throes of a serious depression. Legalized gambling seemed the only way out of the looming crisis.

But for a state which has always had the reputation of "live and let live," coupled with a devil-may-care public attitude, Nevada, surprisingly enough, had more stringent controls on gambling in its infancy than in the prudish 1930's. James Nye, the Nevada Territory's first governor wrote, "I particularly recommend that you pass laws to prevent gambling. Of all the seductive vices extant, I regard that of gambling as the worst. It holds out allurements hard to be resisted; it captivates and ensnares the young, blunts all the moral sensibilities and ends in utter ruin."

The first legislature took the message to heart. Nevada, in the very center of the western frontier, passed a law making owning or working in a gambling hall a felony! The fine: $5,000. And the people who would frequent gambling establishments were in for trouble as well. To be caught patronizing a saloon which offered gambling was punishable as a misdemeanor and carried a $500 fine! Though the law was tough, it lacked teeth. Officials merely looked the other way, and gambling continued to prosper openly. Not a single establishment or patron was ever fined.

In 1866, Governor Henry Blasdel urged the passage of stricter controls, but he met with resistance as well. A pro-gambling bill was passed which licensed and taxed all operators. Although Blasdel vetoed the bill, the legislature overrode his move, and Nevada's first true gambling bill was officially on the books. Under terms of the legislation, gamblers were allowed to operate for a fee. In Storey County, the state's most populated, the amount was $400 quarterly. A sizeable sum began pouring into government coffers.

From the late 1860's until well after the turn of the century, various interests continued to make a run at the pro-gambling laws. In 1877, "An Act to Prohibit the Winning of Money From Persons Who Have No Right to Gamble It Away," allowed dependent families to serve notice on gambling halls if they were being deprived of personal funds by a hapless gambler. In 1889, the legislature again bowed to political pressure and cut back the number of hours that gambling could be operated. Gambling halls, which had always remained open twenty-four hours a day, were now ordered to shut down between midnight and 6 a.m.

The laws remained relatively untouched until 1909; by that time, anti-gambling forces had gained momentum. They pointed out that gambling houses had followed the booming mines of Tonopah and Goldfield, and cheating was rampant, hurting Nevada's image in the eyes of would-be investors. Reno, the commercial hub of the state, was now run by established businessmen who bowed to religious pressure from the community. A poem was circulated which, for many, said it all:

> O Nevada, Wicked State,
> Cut the gambling ere too late.
> Lift yourself out of the mire;
> Throw the Crap game in the fire.

Anti-gambling forces rallied behind the members of the Methodist Episcopal Church, 12,000 strong. On March 29, 1909, Governor Denver Dickerson signed into a law a bill outlawing gambling in all forms.

The next twenty years would prove crucial for the Silver State. Anti-gambling forces predicted that legitimate industry would flood the state in the wake of gambling's prohibition. It didn't happen. Nevada, sparsely populated, lacked the work force to attract large businesses. Mother Nature would never allow her prominence from an agricultural standpoint. Nevadans looked around and saw a bleak future. By 1931, the business interests had begun to realize that, if Nevada were to survive, gambling would have to be legalized again. Despite the outcry from much of the nation, Governor Balzar signed two monumental bills into law on the same day. The first decreased the waiting period for a Nevada divorce (another attempt to attract tourists), and the other legalized gambling for the second time in the state's history.

The reasons, of course, were many, The very fact that Nevada had such a small population made the control and management of the industry, though slow in coming, quite easy. Second, there was a major construction project taking place in the southern portion of the state in Boulder Canyon. The dam being built, heralded as the largest project ever undertaken on the American continent, was certain to attract construction workers to the sleepy little railroad town known as Las Vegas. With the legalization of gambling, many thought, Nevada could certainly attract scores of Mohammeds to the mountain.

It all came true in the 1950's. Wrote Ralph Roske, "Before 1931, gambling had been an important part of Nevada life, but it was secondary. When Fred Balzar signed that bill into law on March 19, 1931, he was putting in motion forces that would deeply and profoundly affect Nevada's political, economic and social composition from then until now, and far into the future." Legalized gambling in Nevada had finally come to stay.

A Publisher with Flair

Virginia City's *Territorial Enterprise* is the most famous newspaper in Nevada history, at one time boasting the largest circulation in the entire west. During its heyday, it took a chance on a fledgling young writer named Sam Clemens, a.k.a. Mark Twain, and turned him into a genuine American legend. It was more prosperous than many of the city's famous mines. For almost twenty years, beginning in the early 1860's, when the *Enterprise* spoke, the entire nation cocked an ear.

But Nevada was a state of boom and bust, of bonanza and borrasca. Towns sprang up across the desert, and newspapers followed. Just as quickly they both disappeared again, forever hot on the heels of a new discovery, a new strike. By the late 1880's, the glory days of the mines of Virginia City had disappeared. The *Enterprise* managed to hang on tenaciously until 1893, when it closed its doors. It surfaced again the following year, but it never regained the high status of the boom days.

Fast forward now to 1952. The first issue of the "new" *Territorial Enterprise* hit the streets, delivered by seventy-two year old Charlie Addis, who had delivered the paper before it had folded for the second time in 1916. The *Enterprise* was about to be reborn, and, thanks to a flamboyant publisher named Lucius Beebe, it would entice, cajole, and outrage its readers just as it had in the previous century.

Beebe was a character born 100 years too late. Wrote Jake Highton in *Nevada Newspaper Days*, "In his low-crowned, broad-brimmed black hat, string tie, ruffled shirt, black clawhammer coat, frontier pants and boots, he was the glass of fashion on the Comstock. When, thus attired, the publisher of the *Territorial Enterprise* stepped forth into C Street en route to the Delta Saloon for an eye-opener, the tourists were entranced. Here was a character from The Real West. They went away true believers."

Beebe was a graduate from the William Randolph Hearst

school of journalism. Like a character from the motion picture "Citizen Kane," he was born of a wealthy family and raised on a diet of caviar, cigars, and champagne. He attended only the finest Ivy League schools, but found them lacking. Rather than join the ranks of New York's social elite, he chose instead to chronicle their antics. In 1929, he joined the city staff of the New York *Herald-Tribune;* within a few short years, he was more famous than those who frequented his columns.

Wrote Wolcott Gibbs in *The New Yorker:*

> At Yale, it was his merry custom, on returning from week-ends in New York, to attend his first Monday-morning class in full evening dress, wearing a monocle and carrying a gold-headed cane. At Harvard, his room contained a roulette wheel and a bar equipped to make any drink a guest could name. His departure from New Haven (Yale) was partly the result of his appearance at the Hyperion Theater extravagantly bearded and brandishing a bottle and shouting that he was professor Henry Hallam Tweedy of the Divinity School. His stay at Harvard was enlivened by his circulation of a ballot to determine how the college stood on trading President Lowell and three full professors for a good running backfield.

But there was a serious side to Beebe as well. During his career, he wrote more than two dozen books and wrote prize winning poetry. He may have envisioned his migration to the small Nevada mining town of Virginia City when, back in 1923, he penned a poem that began, "I am weary of these times and this dull burden...."

"Beebe may have been the most astonishing, the most bizarre, the most outré figure ever connected with Nevada journalism," wrote Jake Highton. Indeed, his wealth and political connections enabled him to carry on an open homosexual relationship with his editor, Charles Clegg, throughout the 1950's, a time when such relationships were unheard of. He prowled the streets accompanied by a huge St. Bernard, known affectionately as T-Bone Towser, who was equipped with a custom-made brandy cask from Abercrombie and Fitch. Although Towser kept all who came in contact with Beebe at bay, he hardly needed protection. Beebe himself presented a most imposing figure: he stood 6'3" and topped the scales at 220 pounds.

His tolerance for alcohol was legendary. Highton recalled a dinner meeting of the Nevada State Press Association held in Reno in

1953. Beebe arrived late and discovered to his dismay that the bar had been closed by president John Sanford of the *Reno Evening Gazette*. "Beebe loudly demanded his usual martini," wrote Highton. "Incredulous and angry that the great Beebe was denied a drink at the association's own bar, [he] ostentatiously ordered champagne for all the association's tables -- except for the head table where Sanford sat."

As he had in his days with the *Herald-Tribune*, Beebe became more famous than his own newspaper. He maintained an elaborately furnished $325,000 railroad car, aptly named Virginia City, but he apparently did so for no other reason than the fact that he missed the romantic, by-gone days of train travel. He flaunted the car at every occasion, and would eventually write almost a dozen books on the American rail system, including one on the famous Virginia and Truckee Railroad.

Under Beebe's tutelage, the *Territorial Enterprise* rose almost to the heights of its former glory. Although by now most of its readers were from beyond Nevada's borders, for a time it became the largest weekly in the state. Wrote Highton, "The paper was feisty. It had guts. It tangled with all comers, particularly those with 'pretensions to good words or elevated public conduct.' It rejected the notion that a newspaper's obligation is to the public. In a day when newspaper offices were becoming more like banks and insurance companies, [Beebe] kept a high informality and a low passion for the nearby tavern. The *Enterprise* was quoted, envied, and hated."

Highton was right, for other bastions of the Fourth Estate were obviously a bit envious of the raucous Beebe and his "tiny" Comstock publication. Wrote *Newsweek* glowingly, "In all the world there isn't a newspaper remotely resembling the *Territorial Enterprise*."

Lucius Beebe, along with editor/photographer Charles Clegg, kept the *Enterprise* afloat with colorful aplomb for almost a decade. Then, almost as suddenly as he had appeared, Beebe moved on, this time to San Francisco where he wrote a lively column entitled "The Wild West."

Beebe died in 1966, but today there are those in Virginia City who still remember him vividly, though not fondly. "He was an absolute ass!" recalls one old-timer. Perhaps. But the man who was born 100 years too late had managed, at least temporarily, to do the impossible. He had brought the *Territorial Enterprise* and Virginia City back into the spotlight once again. Perhaps it was a feat that could have been accomplished by no one else.

I Hereby Resolve...

As much as things change, just as often they don't, especially where the human animal is concerned. Since man first started thinking, part of that thought has revolved around the idea that he might better himself. So, from time to time, this sentient being examines his life and resolves to change some quality, some behavior, some habit he feels needs improvement. The following New Year's "resolutions" from years gone by are perfect examples.

Jonas Leonard, 1843. "I hereby resolve that when we finally reach the end of this cursed desert, I shall never touch a drop of whiskey again!" Apparently, Jonas had a drinking problem when he reached the Black Rock desert. Sometime later he didn't. God works in mysterious ways.

Oliver Franklin, 1860. "It is with great regret that I hereby promise not to visit Miss Nancy's in the new year." Although this resolution seems quite innocent on the surface, Miss Nancy's was a Virginia City house of ill-repute. History doesn't record the reason for Oliver's sudden abstention.

Forrest Abrams, 1861. "I shall no longer commit vice. I will no longer play whist, faro, or salute the dice. This I pledge for as long as I live." Gosh, I hope Forrest made it past twenty-one.

Abner Stickle, 1862. "I shall not eat beans one hour before bed." Poor Abner. He never heard of Gas-X. Mrs. Stickle probably appreciated his concern though.

Evan Marshall, 1865. "I hereby do promise to write my dearest Mother at least one time in every month. This is the way she will know that I am not daid." You gotta admit, Evan had a point there.

Elizabeth Ralston, 1867. "I have made my resolution for the coming year. I shall partake no more of snuff." That was quite a decision on Liz's part. Inhaling snuff was a very popular and fashionable practice in the 1860's.

Jonathan Aston, 1870. "I vow never more shall I covet my neighbor's wife, nor his daughter." Seems that Jonathan had been quite a rascal up to 1869; age apparently was of no particular concern, either.

Elizabeth Sorenson, 1871. "I have promised Charles that I shall no longer partake of Dr. Fontaine's Remedy and I intend to keep my word." For the uninitiated, the "remedy" referred to was almost pure alcohol. It was a common practice, especially among women who liked to imbibe, to visit the local sawbones rather than a tavern.

Charles Lindsey, 1871. "I have discovered the error of my ways. I shall honor the Sabbath faithfully in the coming year and if I do not lose it at cards, I shall give $10.00 a week to the Orphan's Home." Gosh, for a moment there, I thought old Charley was about to turn over a new leaf.

Georgina Washington, 1871. "I hereby promise that I will not beat the children no more in the next year. I cannot say, however, that I will not beat Thomas." Tom, apparently, was this violent lady's unfortunate husband.

Abigail Georges, 1874. "During the year of our good Lord 1874, I shall say my prayers faithfully each day. I trust God will forgive me if I cannot kneel as well as I used to." Never fear, Abby. God takes His prayers any way He can get them.

James Arnault, 1877. "I shall no longer cuss or fight, or mix with questionable women, and I don't give a damn who knows it!" Jimmy's promise spoke for itself.

Ashford Smythe, 1882. "I hereby renounce evil drink. I indict it as the wild beast of our boasted Christian civilization, untamed and untameable, unwashed and unwashable, uncivilzed and uncivilizable, scattering physical, mental and moral hydrophobia among the people, leaping upon our little children, driving its poisonous fangs into the heart and brain and blood of our young men, stealing the roses from our cheeks and virtue from the hearts of our fathers, breaking the hearts of our mothers, destroying our homes, corrupting our politics, making cowards of the American policeman, perjurers of our public officers, and smiting with the leprosy of perdition the gate of every city and the foundations of every state!" Whew! That was the longest resolution I've ever read. Despite his railings against politicians, this guy probably went on to run for office. At least he knew the language.

Robert Larsen, 1882. "From this day forward I shall drink no more. Drink makes man become a beast and self murderer. I shall no longer drink to other's good health while robbing myself of my own." All right, Bob! See, you can get your point across without resorting to oratory.

William Bonnefield, 1893. "I promise not to cuss or to pull on Virginia's hair. Who wants to pull Virginia's hair, anyway. She is ugly as a mud pie." Although the writer didn't give his age, it's obvious that Bill Bonnefield was quite a precocious youngster. Virginia, on the other hand, probably grew up to be a gorgeous silent movie star.

I hope you've enjoyed these resolutions of years gone by. They bring laughter, tears, some pretty strong emotion. Most important of all, they give us quite a window on what life was like on the early western frontier.

Postscript

Nevada -- she was born of battle during America's bloodiest conflict.

During the westward expansion, which was critical to this country's future, Nevada's mineral wealth fueled a nation poised on the brink of Manifest Destiny.

Today she has carved a world-renown oasis in the desert where the rich and famous, and the not so rich and famous, come to play.

But Nevada is so much more.

One has only to look to her rural areas to see it. Just a short distance from the superhighways and highrise casinos, far from the clatter of slot machines and the cry of the croupier, if you take the time to look for it, you will find the real west.

Despite its reputation for glitz and glamor, Nevada is, as it always has been, primarily a mining state. The cold, hard truth is that once those precious metals have been taken from the ground they can never be replaced. And once the gold and silver are gone, the towns that had sprung up must, by their very nature, disappear as well.

As a result, the state that is richest in minerals is also the richest in ghost towns. Some historians have noted that Nevada has more "dead" towns than live ones. It's true. Some Nevada towns flourished for no longer than just the twinkling of an eye.

Nonetheless, while they lasted they provided a treasure trove of stories of the *real* American West. I hope you've enjoyed some of them...

Norm Nielson
September, 1994

Bibliography

Angel, Myron. *History of Nevada, 1881* (Burbank: Howell North Books, 1858)

Beebe, Lucius, and Charles Clegg. *Legends of the Comstock Lode* (Stanford: Stanford University Press, 1954).

Botkin, B. A. *A Treasury of American Anecdotes* (Gallahad Books, 1992).

Brooks, Juanita. *The Mountain Meadow Massacre* (University of Oklahoma Press, 1964).

Bryant, Edwin. *What I Saw in California* (University of Nebraska Press, 1985).

Carlson, Helen S. *Nevada Place Names* (University of Nevada Press, 1974).

Curran, Harold. *Fearful Crossing: The Central Overland Trail Through Nevada* (Nevada Publications, 1974).

DeQuille, Dan. *The Big Bonanza* (Nevada Publications, 1974).

Doten, Alfred. *The Journals of Alf Doten, 1849-1903* (University of Nevada Press, 1973).

Drury, Wells. *An Editor on the Comstock Lode* (Pacific Books, 1936).

Earl, Phillip I. *This Was Nevada* (Nevada Historical Society, 1986).

Edwards, Elbert B. *200 Years in Nevada* (Publishers Press, 1978).

Erdoes, Richard. *Saloons of the Old West* (Howe Brothers, 1985).

Garrison, Webb. *A Treasury of Civil War Tales* (Rutledge Hill Press, 1988).

Georgetta, Clel. *Golden Fleece in Nevada* (Venture Publishing Company. Ltd., 1972).

Glasscock. G. B. *Gold in Them Hills* (Nevada Publications, 1988).

Higgs, Gerald B. *Lost Legends of the Silver State* (Western Epics, Inc., 1976).

Highton, Jake. *Nevada Newspaper Days* (Heritage West Books, 1990).

Hillyer, Katharine. *Young Reporter Mark Twain in Virginia City*

(Western Printing and Publishing Co., 1964).

Hoig, Stan. *The Humor of the American Cowboy* (University of Nebraska Press. 1958).

Hopkins, Sarah Winnemucca. *Life Among the Paiutes: Their Wrongs and Claims* (Bishop: Sierra Media, Inc., 1969).

Hulse, James W. *Forty Years in the Wilderness* (University of Nevada Press, 1986).

Johnson, Leroy and Jean. *Escape from Death Valley* (University of Nevada Press, 1987).

Lewis, Oscar. *Silver Kings* (University of Nevada Press, 1986).

Lewis, Oscar. *The Town That Died Laughing* (University of Nevada Press, 1986).

Lingenfelter, Richard E., and Richard A. Dwyer. *Death Valley Lore* (University of Nevada Press, 1988).

McDonald, Douglas. *Virginia City and the Silver Region of the Comstock Lode* (Nevada Publications, 1982).

Mathews, Mary McNair. *Ten Years in Nevada or Life on the Pacific Coast* (University of Nebraska Press, 1985).

Miller, Max. *Reno* (Dodd, Meade, 1941).

Mills, W. S. *The Press Letter Book of Southwest Mining and Milling Company* (1892).

Murbarger, Nell. *Ghosts of the Glory Trail* (Nevada Publications, 1956).

Nielson, Norm. *Reno: The Past Revisited* (Tales of Nevada Publications, 1988).

Nielson, Norm. *Tales of Nevada* (Tales of Nevada Publications, 1989).

Nielson, Norm. *Tales of Nevada, Vol. 2* (Tales of Nevada Publications, 1990).

Oldham, Willa. *Carson City* (Desk Top Publications, 1991).

Olds, Sarah E. *Twenty Miles from a Match* (University of Nevada Press, 1978).

Ralli, Paul. *Nevada Lawyer* (Murray and Gee, Inc., 1949).

Rice, George Graham. *My Adventures With Your Money* (Nevada Publications, 1986).

Rocha, Guy, and Jeffrey Kintop. *The Earp's Last Frontier* (Great Basin Press, 1989).

Scott, Lalla. *Karnee, A Paiute Narrative* (University of Nevada Press, 1984).

Seagraves, Anne. *Women Who Charmed the West* (Wesanne Publications, 1991).

Stone, Irving. *Men to Match My Mountains* (Doubleday, Inc., 1956).

Taylor, Jock. *One Hundred Years Ago in Nevada* (Western Sales Distributing, Inc., 1964).

Thompson, David. *Nevada Events: 1776-1985* (Cal-Central Press, 1987).

Twain, Mark. *Mark Twain in Virginia City, Nevada* (Nevada Publications, 1985).

Wheeler, Sessions S. *Paiute* (University of Nevada Press, 1986).

Williams III, George. *Mark Twain: His Adventures at Aurora and Mono Lake* (Tree By The River Publishing, 1985).

Williams III, George. *Mark Twain: His Life in Virginia City, Nevada* (Tree By The River Publishing, 1985).

Williams III, George. *Mark Twain: Jackass Hill and the Jumping Frog* (Tree By The River Publishing, 1985).

Index

Russell, W.H., 33-34
Saloons of the Old West, 79, 80
Sandstorm (mine), 150-51
Sazerac Lying Club, 116-17
Schussler, Herman, 101-03
Seagraves, Anne, 195
Searchlight, 120, 177-78
Searcy, Fred, 181-83
Sharon, William, 50-51, 112, 129
Silver Bow Standard, 190
Siston, Jim, 46
Smith, Thomas, 72
Stewart, Helen, 174
Stimler, Harry, 149-51
Stone, Irving, 77
Summerhayes, Martha, 119
Sutro, Adolph, 111-13
Swayze, H.F., 84-85
Tahoe, Lake, 42, 102, 107-09
Territorial Enterprise, 49, 51, 54, 66, 115, 116, 139, 201, 203
Thomas, Jeremiah, 169
Thompson, John A., 45-47
Tonopah, 98, 141, 143-47, 149-51, 156, 198
Truckee, Chief, 9, 24
Twain, Mark, 42-43, 49, 51, 53-55, 65-69, 101, 107, 115, 139, 169
Wabuska Mangler, 139
Walker, Joseph Reddeford, 5-7
Wilkins, Laura, 185-87
Williams III, George, 49, 50, 55
Wingfield, George, 150, 165-67
Winnemucca, Chief, 42, 59, 123
Winnemucca, Sarah, 123-25
Wright, Frank, 174, 178
Yellow Jacket (mine) 112
Young, Brigham, 14, 25-27, 173